daily GREENS
4-DAY CLEANSE

Jump-Start Your Health,
Reset Your Energy,
and Look and Feel
Better than Ever!

Shauna R. Martin
Creator of Daily Greens Beverages

Foreword by Mayim Bialik

Race Point
PUBLISHING

DEDICATION

I dedicate this book to all the young breast cancer warriors out there. Live life like you mean it!

In memory of all the fallen cowgirls (young women who have lost their battle with breast cancer). You may be gone from this earth, but you will not be forgotten.

In honor of and in memoriam to my sisterhood of fellow breast cancer warriors, 1 percent of the royalties from this book will be donated to programs that provide support and services to young women battling breast cancer.

....

Race Point Publishing
A division of Quarto Publishing Group USA Inc.
142 West 36th Street, 4th Floor
New York, NY 10018

RACE POINT PUBLISHING and the distinctive Race Point Publishing logo are trademarks of Quarto Publishing Group USA Inc.

Text copyright © 2015 by Shauna R. Martin

Photography copyright © 2015 by Quarto Publishing Group USA Inc.
Photography copyright © Shutterstock: pp. 46, 47, 49, 50, 51, 53, 56, 78, 105, 106, 125, 136, 137, 139
Photograph by Brenda Ladd: p.11

ISBN: 978-1-63106-032-8

PHOTOGRAPHY: Bill Milne (www.billmilne.com)
EDITORIAL DIRECTOR: Jeannine Dillon
PHOTOGRAPHY SHOOT ART DIRECTION: Heidi North
MANAGING EDITOR: Erin Canning
COPY EDITOR: Lindsay Herman
NUTRITIONAL CONSULTANT: Ian Stern, DC, CCN (www.drianstern.com)
COVER AND INTERIOR DESIGN: Karla Baker (www.karlabaker.com)

Library of Congress Cataloging-in-Publication data is available

Printed in China

10 9 8 7 6 5 4 3 2 1

www.racepointpub.com

contents

4   *Foreword*

6   *Introduction*

9   *Preface*

14   **CHAPTER 1** *Before You Cleanse*

34   **CHAPTER 2** *New Year 4-Day Green Juice & Raw Food Cleanse*

62   **CHAPTER 3** *Spring 4-Day Green Juice & Raw Food Cleanse*

90   **CHAPTER 4** *Summer 4-Day Green Juice & Raw Food Cleanse*

118   **CHAPTER 5** *Fall 4-Day Green Juice & Raw Food Cleanse*

148   **CHAPTER 6** *Maintaining Post-Cleanse*

172   *Acknowledgments*

174   *Index*

foreword

In my almost forty years on the planet, I have seen many eating and dieting trends come and go. No fat, low fat, high protein, no carbohydrates, raw, only cauliflower soup. . . . You name it, and people have tried it! However, what remains consistently recommended by leading doctors of every persuasion is that we need to eat fewer processed foods, more fruits and vegetables, and more foods in their natural state. Period.

I have been vegan for almost seven years and was vegetarian for twenty years before that. I ate pretty healthily, but I have a confession to make: Since becoming a mom almost ten years ago, I have gotten in the habit of grabbing a handful of chips or pretzels or cookies here and there. Well, the "here and there" had lodged itself literally here and there, mainly around my hips and belly. This Mama had accumulated a little bit too much "here and there" . . . here and there.

This past year, I heard about juicing as a way of life, and honestly, it sounded weird, even though it held the possibility of helping me get rid of my "here and there," among other benefits. When I heard about Daily Greens through its founder, Shauna, her story really inspired me. I could relate to her perspective as a young mom who wanted to improve her health and designed these juices from that desire, but her experience battling cancer was really what touched me. I felt empowered because of her dedication and her motivation not only for her health, but for the health of others.

I had some concerns about attempting a juice cleanse despite all of my optimistic posturing. Although I never considered myself to have an unhealthy relationship with food, as I prepared to start the cleanse, I started to feel a sense of panic and impending doom. I felt like food was being taken away from me forever (even though that makes no logical sense!). Thankfully, I was able to acknowledge that these kinds of fears and this kind of panic were things that I could cleanse as well.

To make a four-day-juice-cleanse-story short, the juices tasted good enough that I didn't feel like I was being punished by drinking them. I snacked on raw stuff like fruits and veggies throughout the day. I simply wasn't hungry or grumpy at all. I felt full of energy. Simple foods started tasting really good to me, and that hasn't gone away even months after I've finished the cleanse.

I felt so good after my four-day cleanse that I kept going. I ended up eating raw for nine whole days, with one or two juices a day. I lost weight off my hips and tummy and can fit into my old jeans again!

I took a chance and was inspired enough to commit to disciplining my eating for four days. It transformed my palate, made my body healthier, and put me back in control of my eating and my relationship with food.

If that's trendy, count me in.

—Mayim Bialik

introduction

In the spring of 2007, I experienced sudden weakness and some numbing on my left side: leg, arm, and midsection. At first, I thought I had experienced a stroke, but after two MRIs and other tests it was determined that I had sclerotic scar tissue on my brain—a sign of multiple sclerosis (MS). When the official diagnosis came in, I was both scared and shocked. MS did not run in my family, and I had experienced no health problems before this. What was I supposed to do? How could I slow the progression? I was only in my early twenties, and as a registered dietician and nutritionist, I was familiar with the painful progression of MS in patients who had been diagnosed with the disease.

It has been almost eight years since the diagnosis, and I am proud to say that I am practically symptom-free. I attribute it to the power of raw foods and daily green juices in my life! After the scar tissue was discovered on my brain, I turned to nutrition for help. I began incorporating more raw produce into my diet, focusing mostly on leafy greens and other nonstarchy vegetables. I completed a juice cleanse very similar to the Daily Greens 4-Day Cleanse and began replacing toxic food-like products and processed foods with raw fruits and veggies and other whole foods. Within a few months' time, my symptoms began to improve. Hip and back pain and tightness went away, as did the exhaustion and migraines. I felt stronger and more alert, I was able to complete my workouts successfully, and I was able to maintain balance and increase strength on my left side. I was amazed at the results. Since then, raw produce, green juices, and green tea (another great brain booster and source of antioxidants) have become part of my daily routine. Even when I'm traveling, I try to get in as much as I can. Oh, the power of raw food!

The Daily Greens 4-Day Cleanse is a gentle, nourishing way to rid your body of unwanted toxins, and it may help reduce your risk of chronic diseases. I not only claim this with my background in clinical nutrition, but also out of my personal experience. There are many ways to cleanse your body and get rid of the toxin buildup there, but not all cleanses are created equal. Some are more effective and efficient than others, and the Daily Greens 4-Day Cleanse belongs in the former category.

THE KEYS TO A SUCCESSFUL CLEANSE

ANTIOXIDANTS

Consuming a variety of antioxidants is essential to cleansing well. Antioxidants protect your cells from free radicals, which can damage cells and even cause them to die. It is important that you consume a variety of antioxidants because each type of antioxidant serves a specific purpose, targeting specific cell groups and body systems. The Daily Greens 4-Day Cleanse incorporates a wide range of fruits and vegetables that provide you with a broad repertoire of vital antioxidants to support and improve your body's cleansing process.

HYDRATION

Adequate hydration is essential to cleansing well. The 4-Day Cleanse ensures that you stay hydrated with lemon water and green tea when you first wake up, the three green juices throughout the day, and plenty of cool, fresh water. All these fluids will assist the kidneys and intestines in moving the toxic buildup out of your body.

GIVE YOUR DIGESTIVE TRACT A BREAK

Health-care professionals frequently stress the need for whole grains and protein in our diets, as well as noting the beneficial resveratrol in wine and the mental benefits of caffeine. So why should we remove these items during the 4-Day Cleanse? While it's true these foods and substances provide valuable nutrients or benefits on a daily basis, they can place a heavy digestive burden on your body. In fact, did you know that digestion can require as much as half of your body's available energy on a daily basis? Animal protein in particular requires increased energy to be broken down so the available nutrients can be absorbed. Additionally, with mass agricultural practices as they are today, many animal proteins, alcoholic drinks, and sources of caffeine contain hormones, chemicals, and additives that add to the buildup of toxins in your body. The Daily Greens 4-Day Cleanse gives your digestive tract a break by incorporating simple juices throughout the day that require the expenditure of less energy in the digestive tract. So raw fruits and veggies can be consumed as needed, decreasing the energy required for digestion and allowing it to be funneled elsewhere—like recharging your body!

THE RAW DIFFERENCE

Raw fruits and vegetables naturally contain large amounts of vitamins, minerals, antioxidants, digestive enzymes, and phytonutrients. When fruits and vegetables are cooked, many of these vital nutrients are lost, either through heat or water, decreasing the concentration of nutrients in a given amount of fruit or vegetable. While incorporating some cooked fruits and veggies on a regular basis is perfectly fine, it is important to maximize your body's cleansing process with a high intake of raw fruits and veggies. The consumption of specific raw foods during your cleanse can potentially decrease some of the negative side effects that often accompany cleanses and detox diets, like headaches, fatigue, and stomachaches.

What makes the Daily Greens 4-Day Cleanse different from many other cleanses is that it incorporates raw foods high in fiber, plant protein, and healthy fats at the end of each day for your dinner meal. Many cleanses simply provide your body with the tools to gather toxins from your body's tissues and move them into your digestive tract; however, a vital part of successful cleansing is the elimination of those gathered toxins from your body altogether. Fiber does just that. It provides the bulk, or the "glue," to help your digestive tract bind and eliminate the toxic buildup. Without consuming fiber at the end of the day, the gathered toxins will sit in your digestive tract. This can potentially cause cellular damage to your tract and other bodily tissues, as well as constipation and unnecessary digestive discomfort. You might even know someone who has tried a cleanse and has complained about headaches, skin breakouts, or irritability. Eliminating the gathered toxins at the end of each day on the Daily Greens 4-Day Cleanse will allow your body to expunge maximum buildup without causing unnecessary discomfort.

After completing the 4-Day Cleanse, you should feel light, energized, and de-bloated. Your digestion will be easier and improved (as will your bowel movements), and you'll likely get a better night's sleep. Providing your body with nutrients in their natural, raw form is ultimately fueling your body to cleanse and heal as it needs to. Your body is an incredible machine! Feed it well, and enjoy the energy and life you get in return.

—*Lauren Minchen, MPH, RDN, CDN*

preface

I vividly recall sitting on the floor of my shower with water and tears streaming down my face trying to figure it all out. I could not stop thinking . . . why? Why me? What did I do wrong? On July 28, 2004, my son's first birthday, I had been diagnosed with breast cancer at the age of thirty-three. And then, just a few weeks later, my younger sister was also diagnosed with breast cancer at thirty-one years old.

Happier periods of my life started flashing through my mind as I sat in that shower. I remembered racing with my younger sister through banana plantations by a house we lived in during a four-year stint in Puerto Rico. We were probably eight and ten years old at the time, and I recall running barefoot through the trees, stopping to pick a banana or an orange here and there. Sometimes we would gather mangoes and avocados to take back to our mother to serve with dinner. As I sat on my shower floor mourning the loss of my breasts, I tried hard to remember. Didn't I also recall plantation workers spraying down those banana trees with pesticides? Were those pesticides the reason why my sister and I came to have aggressive breast cancer, mine having grown unchecked into stage II breast cancer while I breastfed my son for nine months?

I flashed-forward a number of years to my grandmother's garden in Arkansas. My sister and I spent many happy hours helping her plant and pick tomatoes, okra, cucumbers, and all kinds of other wonderful vegetables. Again, I strained to remember that pesticide she used to put on the vegetables to keep the bugs away. What was it called? Sevin dust? Weren't we told that we had

to keep the cats away from it for fear of their ingesting it and dying from it? I remember Grandma hollering at us not to eat the vegetables until she had a chance to wash off the "poison," and even the Centers for Disease Control reported in a study that a single dose of 250mg consumed by an adult male resulted in "moderate poisoning." Was this why we had breast cancer? Had we eaten fruits and vegetables covered in poisonous pesticides that later settled in our breast tissue to form cancer cells? Was that possible?

I started thinking about our college days and the TV dinners heated with plastic wrap and consumed quickly while in the midst of cramming for exams. Was it all the chemicals in the processed food that we ate?

We had no family history of breast cancer until we were both simultaneously diagnosed with the disease—years before our doctors would normally start screening us for breast cancer. In fact, no one in our immediate family had ever had any type of cancer. I had been to at least a half-dozen doctors who really had no answer for the "why." Most agreed that it was probably somehow genetic, although they admitted they were stumped by the fact that both my sister and I had tested negative for the known genetic mutations for breast cancer. Most of the physicians that I saw just threw up their hands and said we would probably never know the cause. They confirmed that not enough information is known about the genetic predisposition to breast cancer and certainly not enough information is known about the environmental and food-supply factors that could potentially cause breast cancer.

"We had no family history of breast cancer until we were both simultaneously diagnosed...."

One thing the doctors did all seem to agree upon was that our treatment plans should be the most aggressive available. Before all was said and done, we each underwent a year of mind-numbing chemotherapy, double mastectomies, and multiple surgeries to reconstruct our breasts. Due to my advanced breast cancer, all of my lymph nodes had to be removed from under one of my arms, leaving me with lymphedema (swelling caused by poor drainage of lymph fluid) in my left arm, hand, and torso, which I will have for the rest of my life. Then, after six years of hormone therapy, my team of doctors advised me that I should also remove my ovaries to eliminate the risk of more breast cancer or, even worse, ovarian cancer. So at the age of thirty-nine, I had both ovaries removed, putting my body into premature and permanent menopause.

Prior to our breast cancer diagnosis, my sister and I were the pictures of health. We were raised as vegetarians by our military doctor father and our registered nurse mother, who are both very health conscious and taught us to eat right, exercise daily, and watch our weight. We have never been even remotely obese, smoked a cigarette, or touched a piece of red meat (all the supposed top risk factors for breast cancer). So again, I had to ask, why?

THE JOURNEY FOR ANSWERS

It has now been over nine years since that fateful day when my doctor told me I had breast cancer, and I finally know the answer to the "why?" I was meant to have breast cancer so that I would go on a journey in search of answers. That journey would not only change my life, but also allow me to educate others, to assist in the growing movement to change the way America thinks about food and diet.

The first part of my journey for answers entailed reading everything I could get my hands on about the connection between food and disease, and in particular the connection between food and cancer. On my required reading list were *The China Study*, by Dr. T. Colin Campbell and Thomas M. Campbell II, and Michael Pollan's *The Omnivore's Dilemma* and *In Defense of Food*. I learned from Dr. Campbell that there was likely a connection between the foods I had consumed and my untimely breast cancer. Dr. Campbell's fifty-year study of rural populations in China provides evidence of a direct connection between not only the consumption of animal products and cancer, but also between the overconsumption of animal products and a host of modern diseases currently plaguing the Western world, including heart disease, obesity, and autoimmune diseases.

From Michael Pollan, I learned the history of how we have applied the principles of Ford's mass production of cars to the mass production of food, which led to McDonald's and the proliferation of fast food in the US. Mr. Pollan educated me on the compromises made in the growing of food and the raising of animals in order to satiate the world's ever-growing demand for fast and processed foods—these compromises include the proliferation of genetically altered versions of our most consumed crops and animals, along with the introduction of pesticides and antibiotics to our food sources and onto our dinner plates. I realized that much of what I had been putting into my body for the first thirty-three years of my life was likely laden with pesticides or packaged with numerous chemical preservatives to create years of shelf life. I had been eating a diet that, while healthy by the measuring stick of the Food and Drug Administration and other government standards, was possibly a contributing factor to my breast cancer.

I gained further inspiration from Kris Carr and her *Crazy Sexy Cancer* movie and books, which chronicle her journey from an incurable cancer into remission through her consumption of a raw, plant-based diet. I realized, with hope, that there might be some explanations as to why cancer had started to grow in my young body. While I was vegetarian for the most part, I overconsumed dairy products and processed foods. We are the only mammal that consumes the milk of another mammal, and as it turns out, our bodies do not process it very well. Dr. Campbell's studies showed a link between overconsumption of cow's milk products and cancer.

I will never forget the first time I got my hands on Kris Carr's first book, *Crazy Sexy Cancer Tips*, which included a short but powerful chapter on food. It contained an overview of her diet recommendations, and there was a picture that jumped out at me from the page: It showed the first and, at the time, only juice bar in Austin, and the establishment's sign read simply: "Disease Can't Fight Oxygen and Light." Tears streamed down my face as I realized that I may have finally found something in my own crazy breast cancer journey that was under my control. I did not choose breast cancer, nor would I have chosen to remove my breasts and ultimately my ovaries in my thirties. But when you have a small child and a loving husband, you do whatever it takes to stay alive for them. You do what your doctors tell you to do, even if that means poisoning your body with toxic chemotherapy and removing all the offending body parts that harbor cancer. Finally, I had found something that was completely under my control and within my power. From my research, I believed that I could not only heal my body from breast cancer treatment, but I could also help prevent a recurrence of my breast

Shauna with husband Kirk and son Cooper.

cancer. I was sold. I was willing to try anything that could increase the chances that I would be around to see my beautiful son, Cooper, grow up. I would become vegan, and even consume a diet of only raw vegan foods, if that was what it would take to get me healthy. I would start drinking a green juice every morning. I would eliminate all animal products from my diet, including my beloved cheese.

> **"When you have a small child and a loving husband, you do whatever it takes to stay alive. . . ."**

GETTING STARTED

I dove into the deep end, immediately ordering a simple two-speed Breville juice fountain. I will never

Sisters Tamara and Shauna.

coffee and dropped it in favor of green tea. I also realized that I did not need anything else to eat until lunch. This created a mini juice fast each day, from dinner the night before until I ate solid food at lunch the next day. I found that this daily mini-fast helped my body to cleanse itself of toxins from bad eating. Nine years later, I still drink a green juice every day. I am convinced that it has changed the outcome of my life. I am not just surviving my breast cancer, but thriving in every way. I have more energy

forget making my first green juice in my kitchen. My husband, Kirk, thought I was crazy. It was so green, but the smell of the "real" fruits and vegetables coming from my juicer was intoxicating. At first, I put an entire apple in my green juice each morning, but as time went by, I noticed that I was losing the sweet tooth that I had been known for my entire life (I never skipped dessert). The apple started tasting too sweet, so I gradually used less and less until I left it out altogether, drinking a simple combination of kale, cucumber, and celery. I would juice 32 ounces of these ingredients and head out the door each morning with what my friends came to call my "pond water."

The results of drinking a simple green juice every day were amazing. I had an incredible amount of energy all the time. My immune system—which had been completely wiped out by the chemotherapy—rebounded. My skin glowed, and my hair (which was finally growing back) was black and shiny once again. Mentally, I was sharp and clear. And I was happy. For me, the daily flush of nutrients from my green juice was like the fountain of youth.

Over time, I realized that I no longer needed

and drive than many of my friends and counterparts my age. I also require far less exercise to maintain my weight than my friends of a similar age. While I absolutely love and enjoy exercise, I work out regularly to feel good mentally and physically, not to maintain my weight. My weight is maintained by the smart food choices I am making. Since my body fully absorbs the nutrients consumed, I do not constantly feel hungry, and as a result, I naturally only consume the calories needed to maintain a normal weight. My eyesight is also still remarkable. Despite the fact that I am at the age when most start using readers, I can still see perfectly without glasses.

Perhaps the most important thing I know with every fiber in my body is that I will not only be around to see my son Cooper grow up, but also to grow old with my husband. Unfortunately, breast cancer is one of those dreaded diseases from which you are never considered cured. It can rear its ugly head at any time, and often does for those of us diagnosed at such young ages. For that reason, I always stay the course. Each day when I drink my daily green juice, I reaffirm my dedication to my diet, to my healthy way of life, and to staying alive for

Cooper and Kirk. They need me. Plain and simple. I am so blessed to be able to share my story and the healing power of green juice with the world. I am confident that this is the answer to the "why."

PAYING IT FORWARD

After years of spreading the gospel about drinking a daily green juice to my friends and family, in 2012, I decided that it was time to get serious about "paying it forward." Many of my friends and family members had already purchased juicers and started making a green juice every morning. While they all agreed that the health benefits they experienced were undeniable, after a few months they would ultimately put the juicer away, declaring that it was "too hard," "too messy," and "took too much time." I soon realized that if I was going to keep my friends and family drinking a daily green juice, I was going to have to make it for them. So on December 1, 2012, I made sixty bottles of cold-pressed green juice and took it to the local farmers market in Austin, Texas. It sold out in less than two hours. So the next weekend, I made sixty more bottles and did it again. At the time, I was still working my day job as a corporate attorney, so I had to rope in my then-eight-year-old son and husband to help hand-label the bottles and support me at the farmers market. After selling out at two consecutive farmers markets, I realized that there was a serious need for ready-to-drink green juice made the way I make it (with mostly greens, low in fruit, and with no water added). In 2012, fresh green juice was only available in cities that were lucky enough to have a juice bar—or in New York and along the West Coast, where a small number of cold-pressed juice companies had launched locally. I made it my mission to get a green juice into the hands of every American every day. And so it was that my company, Daily Greens, was born. After four short

months, I left my corporate attorney job behind and dove headfirst into the business of making green juice available to anyone and everyone who would listen to me. Only five months after taking that very first batch to the farmers market, Daily Greens launched at Whole Foods Markets—and the rest is history. Today, Daily Greens juices are available coast to coast in thousands of retail outlets. See the website to find the location closest to you: www.drinkdailygreens.com/location.

During my own battle with breast cancer, I cofounded an organization in Texas known as the Pink Ribbon Cowgirls. It is a program that provides a social network and support services to young women battling breast cancer. The concept grew out of the support and companionship my sister and I were able to provide to each other during our two years of treatment together. Over the years, the Pink Ribbon Cowgirls have provided support and sisterhood to hundreds of young women battling breast cancer. Resources for such women are still scarce in this country—despite the increase of breast cancer in young women. For this reason, we set aside a portion of the revenues at Daily Greens to help fund organizations that provide services to young women fighting breast cancer. In order to further this vision and mission, we will also be donating 1 percent of the royalties from this book to those organizations. If you have been touched by someone courageously battling breast cancer, I encourage you to visit our website and see how you can make a difference too: www.drinkdailygreens.com/we-give-back/.

I no longer ask myself, "Why me?" I know now that it was my destiny to battle breast cancer at thirty-three. It made me who I am today. It created in me a burning desire not only to help other young women facing this disease, but to help you, the reader of my book, to get healthy and stay healthy so you can thrive for the important people in your life.

CHAPTER 1

before you
CLEANSE

Before you begin your 4-Day Cleanse, take the time to read this chapter in order to get an overview of cleansing in general, as well as to learn the basics of the meal plan and the equipment you'll need for juicing. Note that you should start preparing your body for the cleanse at least one week prior to beginning it: I've provided seven delicious green breakfast smoothie recipes (see pages 24–31) that will help get your system accustomed to juice fasting and your palate used to "green" flavors. I have also highlighted the foods and beverages you will be eliminating during the cleanse and explained why doing so is important.

Note that the Daily Greens 4-Day Cleanse is safe for most people who are in good health. However, if you are immune-compromised, pregnant, breastfeeding, or suffering from a chronic illness or ongoing health problem, doing a cleanse may not be safe for you. For this reason, I highly recommend that you consult your physician before starting the cleanse if any of these situations apply to you, or if you have any health issues, questions, or concerns about the safety of cleansing.

WHY JUICE?

It was common for our ancient ancestors to eat up to six pounds of leaves per day. But in modern-day throwback "hunter-gatherer" diets, much emphasis is placed on the "hunting" of meat by our ancestors, and we forget that wild game kills were few and far between. While our ancestors mostly subsisted on leaves, berries, and nuts, today the standard American diet consists mostly of animal protein. According to a 2010 study by the Produce for Better Health Foundation, only 8 percent of individuals get the recommended portion of fruits and only 6 percent manage to consume the recommended daily intake of vegetables. But these foods provide vital nutrients needed to fight disease and maintain good health. What's more, the majority of the standard American diet consists of cooked food, and cooking results in the loss of many of the nutrients in the scarce fruits and vegetables that we do consume. And with our modern, fast-paced lifestyle, who has time to eat six pounds of "leaves" a day?

So what is the solution? Juice! Juicing dark leafy greens, along with other vegetables and some fruit, into a green juice can provide in a single drink many of the nutrients that so many of us are not usually getting. The other benefit of juicing? You are condensing these nutrients into a liquid form that is immediately absorbed by the body, with very few of the nutrients lost through the digestive process.

WHY GREEN JUICE?

Dark leafy greens offer higher concentrations of nutrients than many other vegetables and fruits. They are a rich source of minerals, including iron, calcium, potassium, and magnesium, as well as vitamins, including vitamins K, C, E, and many of the B vitamins. They also provide a variety of phytonutrients, including beta-carotene, lutein, and zeaxanthin, which help protect our cells from damage. Dark leafy greens even contain small amounts of omega-3 fats, which are good for you, playing a role in lowering triglyceride levels.

Perhaps the star of these nutrients is vitamin K. Two cups of dark leafy greens provides more than the minimum daily recommended amount of vitamin K. Research cited by the American Cancer Society has provided evidence that this vitamin may be even more important than once thought—and many people do not get nearly enough of it. Not only is vitamin K essential for normal blood clotting, recent studies suggest that deficient levels of vitamin K are linked to an increased risk of some cancers. In addition, studies have revealed that vitamin K may have a role in keeping bones strong, especially in older people.

You might be wondering: *If dark leafy greens are so great, why not just juice kale?* Well, put simply, because it tastes like crap. However, by combining dark leafy greens with other green vegetables and some fruit and herbs, you can create a green juice that both tastes delicious and is full of nutrients that your body needs for long-term health.

THE TRUTH ABOUT VITAMIN SUPPLEMENTS

Did you know that our bodies absorb over 97 percent of the nutrients contained in raw vegetables and fruit? Compare that to vitamin supplements made in a laboratory, which have an absorption rate of 5 to 25 percent.

One of the most frequent questions I am asked is: If you don't eat meat, how do you get calcium and iron? The answer is simple: I eat plants. Specifically, I consume dark leafy greens every day in the form of green juice and vegetable salads. Dark leafy greens such as spinach, kale, collard greens, watercress, and dandelion greens contain more iron than an equivalent serving of cow's milk while also providing a good amount of calcium.

My doctors require frequent bone-density tests and are always very surprised to note that my bone density is fantastic, given my plant-based diet and refusal to take nutrient and mineral supplements. They always tell me that whatever I am doing with my diet is certainly working and to keep up the good work.

WHY CLEANSE?

You've probably heard diet advice over the past couple of decades indicating that you should be eating very small meals every two or three hours. Sound familiar? But this type of diet doesn't give the digestive tract a break. The theory behind juice cleansing is that it gives the body the opportunity to rid itself of toxins.

THE MINI JUICE FAST: I discovered the first way to detox my body was to conduct a mini juice fast every day. So I replaced my usual breakfast with a green juice—a practice that I continue to this day. On an empty stomach, the juice makes its way through to the intestines in minutes. While I give my digestive system a break from the hard work of digesting solid food in the morning, I also infuse my body with a huge flush of vital nutrients and minerals. My first meal of solid food is always lunch. This creates a mini juice fast of eighteen hours or more each day, from dinner until lunch the following day. Even though I don't consume solid food until lunch or later, I don't experience low blood sugar, hunger pangs, or any of the other symptoms one would expect from skipping a solid breakfast in favor of a low-calorie green juice (my juices are approximately 100 calories or less). The most important benefit of the mini juice fast is that I am full of energy all day long.

MULTI-DAY FASTING: The second way I learned to cleanse and detoxify my body was through periodic longer multi-day juice fasts. At first, I tried just drinking juice for several days in a row, but I quickly learned that this did not work, and it even seemed to make me feel more toxic. Why? Simply because I was not completing the job of actually moving the toxins out of my body. I was juice fasting (only drinking green juice) for long periods of time, and toxins were being pulled out of my cells and into my bloodstream, but I was not moving them out of my body through my bowels. As a result, those toxins were accumulating in my bloodstream and giving me horrible detox symptoms including headaches and flu-like symptoms. If I wanted to continue the juice fast, my options at this point were either: 1) take a large fiber pill each day to help move my bowels, or 2) subject myself to a lower intestinal colonic to assist in the process. But neither of these options appealed to me at all.

So I came up with a third option. I decided to consume only green juice during the day, but at night I would eat a raw vegetable dinner. Raw vegetables are digested very quickly, allowing the body to quickly get back to fasting and cleansing. I realized that the benefit of a raw vegetable dinner as part of a healthy cleanse was twofold: First, it allowed me to actually eat something during my multi-day cleanses, providing vital energy to help me function. Second, all the roughage and fiber from dinner prompted my bowels to move and expel the toxins that had accumulated during the day. Since fruit also moves through the digestive tract very quickly, I added small amounts of fruit (or raw vegetables) during the day to maintain a healthy blood sugar level and sustained energy levels. So while I was flooding my body with large quantities of nutrients and minerals from my green juice, I was simultaneously collecting toxins from my body and getting rid of them. And I was accomplishing all of this by simply consuming raw plants. No supplements, no processed foods, no added anything. Isn't simplicity a beautiful thing?

AN OVERVIEW OF THE DAILY GREENS 4-DAY SEASONAL CLEANSES

During your 4-Day Cleanse, you will drink three green juices daily while eating sufficient raw fruits and vegetables to maintain a normal level of energy throughout the day. This will create an extended period of fasting throughout the day that will allow your body to start gathering up and expelling toxins (the juice does not count as food since it will immediately assimilate into the bloodstream when consumed on an empty stomach). Because the green juice recipes in this book are low in sugar, you may need to consume additional fruit or vegetables to maintain a normal level of blood sugar and sufficient energy to go about your daily routine. Note that you should also drink plenty of water throughout the day as you don't want to get dehydrated. Plus, drinking water will assist in flushing out toxins from your body.

For each seasonal cleanse, we've provided a selection of delicious green juices that you can make yourself. If making three juices per day sounds like a lot of work (and time you don't have!), feel free to make larger quantities of your morning green juice, or any other green juice recipes you like, and substitute them for your lunch and snack juices later in the day. You can double or triple the recipes on any of these. When making a large batch, store your juice in an airtight container right after juicing, and keep it refrigerated until you are ready to consume. The juice should be consumed within twenty-four hours, as it spoils quickly. Note that the recipes tend to get "greener" as you move through the cleanse, because your

taste buds should be adjusting to more "green" flavor and you should start losing your sweet tooth. For this reason, I strongly encourage you to try a variety of the recipes during your cleanse.

If time and convenience are issues for you, also note that all of the green juices produced by my company, Daily Greens, are low in sugar and can be substituted for the green juice recipes provided. While substituting a bottle of Daily Greens for a homemade juice is a great time-saving measure, I still highly recommend making some of your own green juices as well. You might come up with your own perfect green juice blend!

In the evening, you will prepare a delicious raw vegetable appetizer and salad to eat for dinner. These recipes can all be mixed and matched depending on what you have available in your fridge. I also encourage you to improvise and substitute your own raw vegetable dishes. The idea is simply to consume a big raw vegetable dinner in order to provide your body with sufficient fiber and roughage to get your bowels moving and expel all those toxins that you have accumulated during your day of juice fasting (this may occur immediately or the next morning). Repeat this cycle for three more days, and I promise your body will thank you for it!

WHY EAT SEASONALLY?

Wondering why there are four cleanses, one for each season? I started doing these four-day cleanses every couple of months, and fell into a rhythm of doing one at the beginning of each season. I would do one the first week of January to start off the new year right. I would do another one as soon as spring arrived, feeling the need for a good spring cleaning. I would do one the first week of summer to kick off swimsuit season in style. And I also loved doing a back-to-school cleanse, as I started my fall routines. The different recipes featured in the different seasonal cleanses are based on my own philosophy for consuming fruits and vegetables that are in season or available from my local farmers market. There are three very important reasons to eat seasonally:

1. Ideally, fruits and vegetables are harvested when they are ripe. This is when they contain the highest level of nutrients they will ever contain during their life cycle.

2. Eating foods in season often means that you can select your produce from your local farmer or farmers market and lessen the environmental impact of shipping produce across the country.

3. Finally, eating seasonally will save you money. The price of produce is lower when it is in season and available locally.

ORGANIC PRODUCE

I recommend that your fruits and vegetables be organic to the greatest extent possible. I know they can cost a lot more at the grocery store, but I believe the benefits far outweigh the cost.

1. I find that organic produce tastes better.

2. While there is differing research on the topic, I believe that organic produce contains higher levels of nutrients (the Organic Trade Association at ota.com lists the results of several major scientific studies).

3. Produce that comes from organic farms does not contain pesticides and other poisons commonly used to kill insects and maximize production. As reported by the National Cancer Institute, it is many of these same pesticides that are now being linked to cancer, and which I personally hold responsible for my untimely battle with breast cancer.

4. Another important reason to buy organic is to support organic farmers, as they use sustainable farming practices that protect and rehabilitate the soil, as well as prevent further contamination of our environment by employing natural fertilizers and pest repellents instead of poisonous chemicals that contribute to the contamination of our groundwater, lakes, rivers, and oceans.

If you are on a budget, I would highly recommend that—at a minimum—you consider purchasing organic versions of the produce that appears on the "dirty dozen" list. This is a list of the fruits and vegetables that retain the most residual poisons from pesticides used by non-organic farmers. Below is the 2014 list published by Dr. Andrew Weil, a health expert who is internationally recognized for his views on leading a healthy lifestyle, his philosophy of healthy aging, and his critique of the future of medicine and health care.

Dr. Weil's "Dirty Dozen Plus":

- Apples
- Strawberries
- Grapes
- Celery
- Peaches
- Spinach
- Sweet bell peppers
- Nectarines (imported)
- Cucumbers
- Cherry tomatoes
- Snap peas (imported)
- Potatoes

Plus these two that may contain "highly toxic" insecticides:

- Hot peppers
- Blueberries (domestic)

FOODS TO ELIMINATE

During your cleanse, you will need to eliminate several items from your diet. Some of these will be tough, but do make the effort. You'll be happy you did.

COFFEE

Coffee can be a diuretic causing dehydration, which is counter-productive to your cleanse goal of fully hydrating and cleansing your body. Other negative effects that coffee can have include acid reflux and an increase in heart rate. Coffee can also increase the body's level of the hormone cortisol, which can lower the activity of the immune system.

ALCOHOL

As you've probably suspected, alcohol is not conducive to cleansing. It is dehydrating, spikes blood sugar levels, causes inflammation, and adds "empty" calories that are devoid of nutrients. Drinking alcohol in any form, including wine, is simply not productive during a cleanse.

REFINED AND PACKAGED FOODS

Refined and packaged foods are not usually what I consider "real food," as they contain countless preservatives and added mystery ingredients. As a rule, if a package contains any ingredients that I don't recognize or can't pronounce, I will not buy it. These refined and packaged foods are at the heart of the current food and health crisis we have in America. By eating these instead of whole foods, people are missing out on many of the essential nutrients provided by the latter. Plus, packaged foods often contain potentially harmful ingredients used as preservatives to extend their shelf life. Some of these packaged foods are "fortified" with artificial and chemically based nutrients like iron, calcium, and vitamins, but these are a poor substitute for the nutrients that naturally occur in real

food. During your 4-Day Cleanse, you will enjoy the full benefits of a plant-based diet that is free of artificial additives, and you will see a dramatic difference in your mood and energy level.

ANIMAL PRODUCTS (INCLUDING DAIRY)

Animal protein takes hours to digest and is not conducive to cleansing. It is important to eat foods that digest rapidly to give your intestines a break. Note that animal protein also usually contains toxins from pesticides that are used in the animals' food supply, as well as hormones and antibiotics used to optimize production of animal protein. This places an even greater burden on the body to get rid of the animal toxic waste.

GRAIN PRODUCTS

While cooked whole grains are an important part of a long-term healthy diet, they also take a long time to digest, and for some people, the gluten in many of these (wheat, rye, barley) causes inflammation in the intestines. One of the goals for your 4-Day Cleanse is to reduce inflammation and give your intestines a rest, so it is best to eliminate cooked grains while cleansing.

EQUIPMENT NEEDED FOR YOUR 4-DAY CLEANSE

While you will need a few basic pieces of equipment like a home juicer and a high-speed blender, the 4-Day Cleanse is pretty simple and does not require much preparation. Here is a list of equipment you should make sure you have at home before you start your cleanse.

HOME JUICER

While I own several high-end expensive juicers, I almost always use my simple Breville Juice Fountain to make green juice at home. It is inexpensive in the juicing world, works wonderfully, and is easy to use. I recommend the two-speed version, which will allow you to alter the speed depending on the produce you are juicing. Using the recommended speed will prevent waste. The fountain opening allows you to put larger pieces of fruit and vegetables into the juicer, thus requiring less time for cutting your produce into small portions. It also breaks down into three parts for easy washing. As of late, there are a number of juicers on the market that attempt to bridge the gap between cold-pressed juicers, like the professional-grade Norwalk, and the centrifugal juicers like the Breville. I have experimented with several of these, including the Huron. While they are nice and may extract slightly more nutrients, they do slow down the process of making juice. I encourage you to do some research on the best juicer for your budget.

A word of caution: Do not attempt to use a blender as a juicer. It just cannot be done. A blender retains all the fiber and, thus, works for making a green smoothie, but not a green *juice*.

HIGH-SPEED BLENDER

You will be using a blender to make green smoothies during the week prior to your cleanse (see pages 24–31) and to make raw soups for dinner during your cleanse. As you will see later on, I am very passionate about my Vitamix. I could not live without it. When trying to break down raw produce into a creamy texture for smoothies, I find it is the only blender that truly gets the job done. I know it comes with a high price tag, so feel free to substitute a regular high-speed blender.

COLANDER

Over the course of your 4-Day Cleanse, you will be washing large quantities of fruits and vegetables, both for your juices and for your raw food dinners; a large colander will make this process easier.

SIMPLE GREEN JUICE FORMULA

My hope for you is that once you do a 4-Day Cleanse, you will crave a morning green juice as much as I do. In case you want to experiment with your own recipes, here are some guidelines for the perfect proportions for making a fantastic green juice.

2 parts sweet juicy greens
(celery, cucumber, romaine)

1 part fruit
(apple, watermelon, pear, pineapple)

⅔ part dark leafy greens
(kale, spinach, collard greens)

⅓ part herb
(mint, basil, cilantro, parsley)

SHARP KNIVES

You will also be chopping up large quantities of fruits and vegetables, so a set of sharp knives is highly recommended. If your knives are dull, you can sharpen them yourself or take them to a store that does knife sharpening before you begin your cleanse. Take extra care when using ultra-sharp knives—you don't want to hurt yourself!

SALAD SPINNER (OPTIONAL)

You will be making a big raw salad most evenings, and a salad spinner can make it easier to prepare your greens. If you don't already have one, a colander to drain your washed lettuce will work just fine as a substitute.

SPIRALIZER AND MANDOLIN (OPTIONAL)

These tools can come in handy for preparing paper-thin veggie slices (on the mandolin) or spaghetti-thin vegetable curls (on the spiralizer).

Both are inexpensive and can easily be found online or in retail stores carrying kitchenware.

CLEAN UP YOUR ACT!

There are three key changes in your diet that I highly recommend you incorporate a week prior to starting the 4-Day Cleanse. These are particularly important if you have never cleansed before, and even more important if you are not accustomed to drinking a green juice every day. If you already drink a green juice on a daily basis and consume a diet high in raw vegetables and fruits, then these early preparations will be unnecessary, and you can proceed right away with your 4-Day Cleanse.

PREP TIP #1: SWITCH FROM COFFEE TO TEA

If you drink coffee every day, then I strongly recommend switching to black tea or green tea one week prior to starting your 4-Day Cleanse. This will give you a reasonable dose of caffeine every morning so as to limit your caffeine withdrawal symptoms and let your body start getting used to having less caffeine before you begin the actual cleanse. During your cleanse, you will be drinking green tea, which not only contains less caffeine than coffee but also has the added benefit of providing you with wonderful antioxidants, including high quantities of catechins, which fight and may even prevent cell damage. What's more, some research shows that green tea improves blood flow and helps lower cholesterol.

PREP TIP #2: START DRINKING A GREEN SMOOTHIE FOR BREAKFAST

So now that I have taken away your morning cup of coffee to get your bowels moving, what next? You can start motivating your bowels by filling them with fiber and roughage from raw fruits and vegetables in the form of a thick, delicious green smoothie. I have included a number of fabulous green smoothie recipes in this chapter in order to provide you with a wide variety of options for the week. Note that it is important to swap out your regular breakfast for a green smoothie. This will start to get you accustomed to the "fasting" element of the 4-Day Cleanse so it won't be as much of a shock to your system. Another reason you'll be drinking a green smoothie for breakfast is so you can start developing your "green palate"—your taste for greens. The more consistently you drink green juice, the more you will crave greens and the less you will crave sugar and sweet things.

PREP TIP #3: MOVE MEAT AND GRAINS TO DINNER

Swap out your normal burger or cold cuts at lunch for a raw salad. Any type of raw salad will work, but eliminate animal protein and grains from it. Save the meat and grains for dinner. This will start preparing your body for the new eating routines you will practice during your 4-Day Cleanse. Take note of how you feel eating just raw vegetables and fruits during the day. You should feel energized, since your body is not burdened with channeling so much energy into digesting food all day long, as the raw fruit and vegetables will digest very quickly using only a fraction of the energy.

Note that all of these tips are also great food habits for life. As we will discuss in Chapter 6: Maintaining Post-Cleanse (see page 149), these wonderful habits will help you maintain optimal health following your 4-Day Cleanse.

FREQUENTLY ASKED QUESTIONS

Is cleansing safe for everyone?

No. If you are immune-compromised, pregnant, breastfeeding, or suffering from a chronic disease or ongoing health problem, cleansing may not be safe for you. As such, I highly recommend that you consult your physician before starting the cleanse if any of these apply to you, or if you have any health issues or questions about the safety of cleansing.

Can I continue the cleanse for more than four days?

Yes! This is one of the questions I get asked most frequently. By the fourth day of the Daily Greens Cleanse, most people will start to feel really amazing, and as a result decide they might want to extend their cleanse. I encourage everyone to continue the Daily Greens Cleanse as long as you feel comfortable, and always consult your doctor if you're not sure. I usually end up continuing a few extra days or until I have some social engagement that gets in the way. Mayim Bialik, a star from the hit TV show *The Big Bang Theory* and a vegan diet and lifestyle ambassador, continued the Daily Greens Cleanse for nine days the first time she tried it. When you are ready to break the cleanse, be sure to follow the plan laid out in Chapter 6: Maintaining Post-Cleanse (see page 149).

Should I cleanse when I am pregnant or nursing?

No. One of the problems with cleansing is that the body releases a substantial amount of toxins into the system while it detoxes, and this can be harmful for your baby.

What happens if I can't finish the cleanse?

A cleanse that lasts for four days is what personally feels right for me and this seems to be the magic number for most people looking to reset and recharge. Through years of practice, I have found this to be the most effective time frame for cleansing. However, every person will have his or her own unique response, and I have found that even one or two days of cleansing is a helpful boost to your system. Any decision to move toward a healthier you is a positive one, so congratulate yourself for taking the first step!

Can I work out while I am on the cleanse?

Yes! The Daily Greens 4-Day Cleanse is designed to provide you with sufficient energy to do your normal day-to-day activities, including exercise. I do recommend, however, that during a cleanse you stick with lighter forms of exercise that do not cause increased hunger. You'll have to determine which forms of exercise are right for you, but during a cleanse I try to stick with light strength classes like yoga and barre or light cardio like a short run or spin class.

In my hometown of Austin, Texas, I am well known for this green smoothie. I started making it over nine years ago at the beginning of my own journey back to good health. I used to take a pitcher of it to my workout to share with everyone in my fitness class. They thought I was crazy for asking them to drink a smoothie that was a brilliant shade of green. Plus, my gym already had a smoothie bar—but they made the type of smoothies popular at the time, with berries or bananas, some form of milk (usually cow's milk), and a big scoop of animal-based protein powder. Since they did not make anything that I would drink, I brought my own. Once folks got past the "greenness" of this smoothie, it was a universal crowd-pleaser.

INGREDIENTS

Big handful of spinach (⅔ bunch)

Handful of mint leaves (from 3 to 4 stems)

¼-inch (0.6 cm) piece ginger root

½ banana (fresh or frozen)

½ cup (88g) mango chunks or sliced peaches (fresh or frozen)

½ cup (120ml) filtered water

SHAUNA'S
green smoothie

1 Wash the spinach, mint, and ginger root.

2 Add all ingredients to your high-speed blender or Vitamix, and blend on High until smooth and creamy.

3 Add more water if needed to obtain desired consistency for drinking.

spicy pineapple-kale
SMOOTHIE

This smoothie is nice and green, but has a fun spicy kick to it because of the ginger and cayenne. It will definitely wake up your taste buds first thing in the morning.

INGREDIENTS

3 to 4 kale leaves

Handful of cilantro (coriander) leaves (from 3 to 4 stems)

¼-inch (0.6 cm) piece ginger root

1 cup (165g) pineapple chunks (fresh or frozen)

½ cup (120ml) filtered water

Pinch of cayenne pepper

1 Wash the kale, cilantro, and ginger root.

2 Add all ingredients to your high-speed blender or Vitamix, and blend on High until smooth and creamy.

3 Add more water if needed to obtain desired consistency for drinking.

⏱ TIME SAVER

Most grocery stores carry bags of frozen fruit that are perfect for making smoothies. I try to keep a variety of frozen fruits on hand to assist with quick smoothie making.

simple green
SMOOTHIE

D / G

It does not get any more basic than combining spinach, banana, and orange into a super-simple green smoothie. I love making this one in the winter, when oranges are in season and a bit sweeter. It takes less than five minutes to prepare, so this is a great go-to recipe when you are in a hurry in the morning.

INGREDIENTS

Big handful of spinach (⅔ bunch)

½ banana (fresh or frozen)

1 medium orange or two small oranges

1 cup (235ml) filtered water

1 Wash the spinach.

2 Add all ingredients to your high-speed blender or Vitamix, and blend on High until smooth and creamy.

3 Add more water if needed to obtain desired consistency for drinking.

creamy avocado
SMOOTHIE

Avocados get a bad rap for being high in calories and fat. However, these are the good kinds of fats—the ones that help lower your cholesterol. Even better? Avocado makes a smoothie creamy, filling, and delicious.

INGREDIENTS

Big handful of spinach (⅔ bunch)

½ large avocado or 1 small avocado

½ banana (fresh or frozen)

1 cup (235ml) filtered water (or coconut water if desired)

1 tsp vanilla extract

Dash of cinnamon (optional)

1 Wash the spinach.

2 Remove the meat from the avocado.

3 Add all ingredients to your high-speed blender or Vitamix, and blend on High until smooth and creamy.

4 Add more water if needed to obtain desired consistency for drinking.

glowing skin
SMOOTHIE

D/G

The ingredients in this smoothie all promote beautiful glowing skin, especially the kiwi. If you want to switch things up a bit, it's fun to swap coconut water for regular water. This will add electrolytes to your smoothie while offering a fun tropical taste.

INGREDIENTS

Big handful of spinach (⅔ bunch)

½ large avocado or 1 small avocado

½ banana (fresh or frozen)

2 kiwi

1 cup (235ml) filtered water (or coconut water, if desired)

1 Wash the spinach.

2 Remove the meat from the avocado.

3 Add all ingredients to your high-speed blender or Vitamix, and blend on High until smooth and creamy.

4 Add more water if needed to obtain desired consistency for drinking.

summer greens
SMOOTHIE

This smoothie is great for summer, combining two of my favorite summer fruits: strawberries and peaches. My son loves this one because these are two of his favorite fruits, as well. If you are looking for some extra protein, throw in some ground chia seeds. You will feel full a lot longer.

INGREDIENTS

Big handful of spinach (⅔ bunch)

½ cup (100g) sliced peaches (fresh or frozen)

½ cup (55g) whole strawberries (fresh or frozen), stems removed

1 cup (235ml) filtered water (or coconut water if desired)

1 to 2 tbsp ground chia seeds (optional)

1 Wash the spinach, peaches, and strawberries (if fresh).

2 Add all ingredients to your high-speed blender or Vitamix, and blend on High until smooth and creamy.

3 Add more water if needed to obtain desired consistency for drinking.

kale-grape-melon
SMOOTHIE

Green grapes and honeydew melon combine so well to form a super-sweet base for a smoothie. Again, if you are looking for a boost of protein, add a couple spoonfuls of ground chia seeds. Make sure they are ground up so all the good stuff can be absorbed by your intestines.

INGREDIENTS

3 to 4 kale leaves

½ cup (75g) green grapes (fresh or frozen)

½ cup (90g) cubed honeydew melon (fresh or frozen)

½ cup (120ml) filtered water

2 tbsp ground chia seeds (optional)

1 Wash the kale and grapes.

2 Add all ingredients to your high-speed blender or Vitamix, and blend on High until smooth and creamy.

3 Add more water if needed to obtain desired consistency for drinking.

Unlike the other drinks featured in this chapter, this is a recipe for a green juice, as opposed to a smoothie. So you'll be using your juicer here—not your high-speed blender. When I first began drinking green juices, I had to incorporate a substantial amount of apple to this one to make it appeal to my taste buds. But day after day, I noticed my palate being cleansed of my cravings for sugar, and the apple started to taste sickeningly sweet. After several months of drinking this every morning, I could actually taste every single ingredient in it with a newly refreshed palate, similar to the one I had as a child. I started to really crave my Morning Greens.

INGREDIENTS

½ bunch of kale (or other dark greens, if desired)

1 cucumber

5 celery stalks, bottoms removed (or 1 head of romaine [cos])

to cut the greenness:
¼ lemon, peeled

¼-inch (0.6 cm) piece ginger root

to add flair:
Handful of basil or mint (6 to 7 leaves)

to add sweetness:
½ apple or pear, or ¼ of either or both, cored and cut into pieces

shauna's daily morning greens JUICE

1 Wash all ingredients except lemon (if using).

2 Cut and core the apple or pear (if using) and cut into pieces that will fit through your juicer.

3 Run all ingredients through your juicer, scrape off foam (if desired), and enjoy!

CHAPTER 2

new year
4-DAY GREEN JUICE & RAW FOOD CLEANSE

Is there a better time of year to begin a cleanse? If you're anything like the majority of the world, you've indulged and enjoyed the wonderful foods of the holidays, and you're ready for a cleanse reset. If you're too busy to make all the juices yourself at home, you can substitute any of our cold-pressed juices sold in stores for the homemade recipes in this chapter. You can find the store locations closest to you on our website (www.drinkdailygreens.com).

To make things easier, we've provided a shopping list (on the pages that follow) and broken it up by juice ingredients and raw food ingredients (which you will need for your dinner each night). If you plan to buy ready-to-drink Daily Greens juices for your cleanse, simply skip to the food shopping list.

Not sure where to shop? I love supporting local farmers, so I highly recommend hitting your farmers market to see if you can find the majority of the ingredients there. You will most likely also need to make a quick trip to the grocery store. Happy shopping!

juice shopping list

VEGETABLES	QUANTITY
Carrot	1 large or 2 small
Celery	2 heads
Cucumbers	4 medium
Ginger root	¼-inch (0.6 cm) piece
Green cabbage	1 head
Kale	3 bunches
Romaine (cos)	3 heads
Spinach	1 bunch or 1 small box, prewashed
Swiss chard	1 small bunch
Watercress	1 bunch

FRUIT	QUANTITY
Green grapes (seedless)	1 bunch
Granny Smith apple	1 medium
Grapefruit	1 medium
Kiwi	1 small
Lemon	2 medium
Lime	1 small
Pineapple	1½ whole
Orange	1 medium

HERBS	QUANTITY
Basil	1 bunch
Cilantro (coriander)	2 bunches
Parsley	1 bunch

OTHER	QUANTITY
Blue-green algae (E3Live AFA)	1 small container of powdered supplement
Cayenne pepper	small amount of dried powder
Sea salt (pink Himalayan)	1 shaker of whole crystals
Vanilla extract	1 small vial

food shopping list

VEGETABLES	QUANTITY
Avocados	4 medium
Baby kale	1 box, prewashed
Butter lettuce	1 head
Carrot	5 medium or 1 bag shredded
Cauliflower	1 head
Celery	2 stalks
Cucumber	1 medium
Fennel	1 bulb
Garlic	3 cloves
Ginger root	1-inch (2.5 cm) piece
Green (spring) onion	1 bunch
Romaine (cos)	2 heads
Sprouts	1 small container
Super greens	1 box, prewashed
Tomato	7 medium
Watercress	1 bunch
White onion	1 medium
Zucchini	1–2 small

FRUIT	QUANTITY
Fuji apple	1 medium
Grapefruit	1 large or 2 small

HERBS	QUANTITY
Basil	1 bunch
Cilantro (coriander)	1 bunch
Oregano	1 bunch
Parsley	1 bunch (for garnish)

NUTS/SEEDS	QUANTITY
Pine nuts (raw)	¼ cup (35g)

OTHER	QUANTITY
Agave nectar (raw)	1 small container
Almond butter (raw)	1 small container
Almond oil	1 small container
Apple cider vinegar (Bragg's)	1 small container
Cayenne pepper	small amount of dried powder
Green tea	4 individual servings
Italian spice	small amount of dried spice
Miso paste (raw, white)	1 small container
Mustard (whole-grain)	1 small container
Nori seaweed sheets	1 package
Olive oil (extra-virgin)	1 small container
Pepper (black, cracked)	1 grinder of whole seeds
Sea salt (pink Himalayan)	1 shaker of whole crystals
Soy sauce (nama shoyu)	1 small container

DAY 1

Congratulations on starting your New Year 4-Day Cleanse! It's a time of new beginnings, so start the year off right by ridding your body of all that holiday indulgence. Throughout your cleanse, in addition to consuming the various juices and raw foods presented here, be sure to drink plenty of water over the course of each day to stay hydrated.

BREAKFAST

1 glass of lemon water (12 ounces)

Upon rising, drink a big glass of water with a squeeze of lemon. If you don't mind it, I suggest heating it up a bit. Lemon will help your digestive tract start moving. This will be especially important during the first couple days of your cleanse as you drop your morning coffee.

1 cup of green tea (8 ounces/235ml)

Next, enjoy a hot cup of green tea. The warmth from the tea will also help start moving your digestive tract along, and if you are experiencing caffeine withdrawal, the tea will help quell your headache. Green tea is also full of antioxidants.

new year morning green
JUICE

D/G

Finally, my favorite part of the morning: preparing my Morning Green Juice. As you can probably tell by now, this morning juice is an essential part of my day. And it can be an essential part of yours too! If you prefer to try your own recipe, keep it simple and follow my "Simple Green Juice Formula" (see page 21).

INGREDIENTS

4 to 5 romaine (cos) leaves

2 to 3 kale leaves

¼ pineapple or 1½ cups (250g) pineapple chunks

Handful of cilantro (coriander) leaves (from 3 to 4 stems)

1 Wash the romaine, kale, and cilantro.

2 Top and tail the pineapple, peel it, and cut into pieces that will fit through your juicer.

3 Run all ingredients through your juicer, scrape off foam (if desired), and enjoy!

Kiwi is a fun and unusual choice that gives your green juice a tropical twist. I love incorporating tropical fruits into my juices in the winter to help chase away the winter blues. It makes me feel like I have taken a momentary beach vacation on a faraway island.

Optional lunch addition:
1 kiwi, peeled and quartered. *On the first day in particular, you may be hungry. If your green juice does not satiate you, enjoy this cut-up fruit as part of your lunch.*

INGREDIENTS

½ Granny Smith apple

2 to 3 romaine (cos) leaves

Handful of watercress (⅓ bunch)

¼-inch (0.6 cm) piece ginger root

1 kiwi

kiwi green JUICE

1 Wash the apple, romaine leaves, watercress, and ginger.

2 Peel the kiwi and cut into pieces that will fit through the juicer.

3 Cut and core the apple and cut into pieces that will fit through your juicer.

4 Run all ingredients through your juicer, scrape off foam (if desired), and enjoy!

orange-romaine green JUICE

D/G

Combining orange with your greens offers a healthy boost to the traditional orange juice. It adds loads of vitamin C to your green juice, which is already packed with vitamin A and B vitamins, making this recipe a nutritious (and delicious!) powerhouse.

Optional snack addition:
1 orange, quartered. *Only snack on the fruit if you are not feeling satiated from your mid-afternoon green juice.*

INGREDIENTS

4 to 5 kale leaves

2 to 3 romaine (cos) leaves

Handful of cilantro (coriander) leaves (from 3 to 4 stems) (optional)

1 orange

1 Wash the kale, romaine, and cilantro.

2 Peel the orange and cut into pieces that will fit in your juicer.

3 Run all ingredients through your juicer, scrape off foam (if desired), and enjoy.

Romaine wraps are one of my go-to quick and easy appetizers. You can put all kinds of fun things into a romaine leaf, roll it up, and replicate the flavors of your favorite sandwich, taco, or wrap. I prefer using prewashed heart of romaine, which does not include the outside dark green leaves that tend to be stronger in flavor and a bit bitter. The leaves at the heart are juicier and sweeter—making them ideal for these scrumptious wraps.

INGREDIENTS

5 to 6 heart of romaine (cos) leaves

3 tbsp raw almond butter

1 tsp raw agave nectar

2 medium carrots, thinly sliced or shredded

2 medium celery stalks, thinly sliced or shredded

almond butter
WRAPS

1 Arrange the romaine leaves on a plate and spread ½ tablespoon of almond butter on the inside of each leaf.

2 Drizzle agave nectar over the almond butter.

3 Distribute veggies evenly onto each leaf.

4 To eat, wrap the sides of each leaf inward to cover the filling, and enjoy!

⏱ TIME SAVER

Most grocery stores carry bags of shredded carrots. In addition to my usual supply of carrots, I always keep a bag of these in the fridge to aid in quick assembly of wraps and salads.

Grapefruit is one of my favorite fruits, especially in the winter. It's also low in sugar compared with other fruits. In Texas, we have the most delicious Ruby Red grapefruit that grows all winter long. I keep it on hand at all times during the winter to add to green juices, smoothies, and salads. Kale, of course, is a wonderful winter green, so baby kale is usually available all winter long.

INGREDIENTS

2 cups (134g) baby kale leaves

Handful of watercress (½ bunch), stems removed

1 avocado, thinly sliced

½ fennel bulb, thinly sliced

Handful of basil (6 to 7 leaves), finely chopped

Handful of cilantro (coriander) leaves (from 5 to 6 stems), finely chopped

1 large grapefruit or 2 small grapefruits

1 tsp almond oil

Sea salt and pepper, to taste

winter grapefruit
SALAD

1 Combine the kale leaves and watercress in a salad bowl and toss well.

2 Add avocado and fennel to kale mixture, then add basil and cilantro. Toss gently to combine.

3 Peel the grapefruit and remove meat from the skins, collecting any juice as you do so. Set aside the grapefruit slices.

4 To make the dressing, whisk together the grapefruit juice and almond oil in a small bowl.

5 Pour the dressing over the salad and toss well.

6 Add grapefruit and toss gently, then season with salt and pepper to taste.

⏱ TIME SAVER

Short on time? Most grocery stores now carry pre-washed containers of baby kale leaves.

DAY

2

Day 2 has arrived. I know that yesterday was tough, but today will be better. Your energy will begin to pick up and you will feel less hungry. This is a sign that your intestines are starting to more fully absorb the nutrients from all the raw fruit and veggies in your green juice and your raw food dinner.

BREAKFAST

**1 glass of lemon water
(12 ounces/355ml)**

Like yesterday, when you rise, have a glass of water, preferably heated, with a squeeze of lemon in it. If your bowels did not move yesterday, hopefully this will get things moving.

**1 cup of green tea
(8 ounces/235ml)**

Your need for caffeine should be a bit less today, as you start to gain energy from your green juice.

**1 glass of New Year Morning
Green Juice
(16 ounces/475ml)
(see recipe on page 39)**

Today should be an easier experience with the juicer—hopefully you're getting the hang of it. To help develop your "green palate," I find it best to stick with the same simple green juice each morning.

vanilla-grapefruit green
JUICE

D / G

The vanilla in this green juice provides a nice touch of sweetness without adding calories.

Optional lunch addition:
1 grapefruit, peeled and sliced. *Your need for additional fruit should decrease each day of the cleanse. However, you don't want to run out of energy, so continue supplementing with fruit if your blood sugar is running low.*

INGREDIENTS

1 cucumber

3 to 4 kale leaves

Handful of cilantro (coriander) leaves (from 3 to 4 stems)

½ grapefruit

¼ lime

1 tbsp vanilla extract

1 Wash the cucumber, kale, and cilantro.

2 Peel the grapefruit and lime, and cut each into quarters that will fit through your juicer.

3 Run all ingredients through your juicer and scrape off foam (if desired).

4 Stir in the vanilla, and enjoy this wonderful combination!

Watercress is a favorite green superfood of mine. It grows naturally in springs and along the riverbanks of slow-moving rivers. When I was a young girl, I used to harvest it straight out of the spring on our farm, and my mother would toss it into our salads for a dash of spicy flavor.

Optional snack addition:
1 small bowl of grapes (no more than 10). *Again, only eat more fruit with your green juice snack if you feel hungry or low on energy.*

INGREDIENTS

1 cup (150g) seedless green grapes

Big handful of spinach (⅔ bunch)

1 cucumber, whole

Handful of watercress (⅓ bunch)

Handful of basil (3 to 4 leaves)

watercress green
JUICE

1 Wash the grapes, spinach, cucumber, watercress, and basil.

2 Run all ingredients through your juicer, scrape off foam (if desired), and enjoy!

SUPERFOOD HIGHLIGHT: watercress

Watercress is a great source of antioxidants, vitamin C, beta-carotene, folate, potassium, phosphorous, iron, and calcium. Watercress also shows extraordinary potential in the realm of cancer prevention and management: It can increase the level of antioxidants in the blood and help protect DNA against damage.

Preparing watercress is simple: After trimming the stems, rinse the greens in cold water and dry on a paper towel or in a salad spinner. Use immediately, or store in a closed container in the refrigerator for up to four days. Watercress can take the place of lettuce in any salad, sandwich, or other recipe, and can be used as a nutritious garnish. It also makes a wonderful ingredient in a green juice.

sweet nori
WRAP

A popular pastime among our friends and family is sushi night. Several of us converge on a house and make an evening of it. As the resident vegan, I am charged with making all the vegetable sushi, and this recipe has become a crowd favorite.

INGREDIENTS

2 to 3 nori seaweed sheets

1 Fuji apple, thinly sliced

½ avocado, thinly sliced

1 medium carrot, thinly sliced or shredded

Handful of basil leaves (6 to 7 leaves)

Raw agave nectar, for drizzling

Sea salt, to taste

1 Cut the nori sheets into thirds with kitchen scissors and place on a cutting board with the shiny side down.

2 Distribute apple, avocado, and carrot evenly onto each nori sheet.

3 Add a bit of ripped basil leaf onto each sheet and follow with a drizzle of raw agave nectar.

4 Season with a touch of salt to taste.

5 Wet the edge of one nori sheet and roll up tightly. Repeat with remaining sheets, and serve.

These are such a fun addition to sushi night. Plus, they're very filling. I discovered this recipe after struggling to make vegetable sushi rolls that were not all damp and droopy—a tall order when you eliminate cooked rice from the mix. I substituted a romaine leaf for the rice and found that it adds a wonderful crispy texture to a sushi roll.

INGREDIENTS

3 nori seaweed sheets

6 small heart of romaine (cos) leaves

1 to 2 tbsp raw miso paste

1 avocado, thinly sliced

1 medium carrot, thinly sliced or shredded

½ cucumber, peeled and thinly sliced

1 cup (50g) sprouts (any kind)

Sea salt, to taste

1-inch (2.5 cm) piece ginger root

1 to 2 tbsp raw soy sauce (nama shoyu), for dipping

veggie hand
ROLLS

1 Cut the nori sheets in half with kitchen scissors and place on a cutting board with the shiny side down.

2 Place a romaine leaf on each nori sheet, with the tip of the leaf aligned with the corner of the nori.

3 Coat the inside of each leaf with miso paste.

4 Distribute avocado, carrot, and cucumber evenly onto each nori sheet.

5 Add a few sprouts on top and season with a touch of salt to taste.

6 Wet the edge of one nori sheet and roll up tightly. Repeat with remaining sheets.

7 Peel the fresh ginger root and slice thinly, then arrange on plate as a garnish. Serve with soy sauce for dipping.

⏱ TIME SAVER

Most grocery stores carry premade veggie sushi, but be sure that it does not include cooked rice, which is not consistent with your raw food cleanse.

DAY 3

Welcome to Day 3 of your cleanse. You should really have the hang of things now. You should also start to experience increased mental clarity as your body continues to eliminate toxins. Your intestines should be getting into more of a rhythm, as you develop new habits. By Day 3, you might also start noticing an awakening of your taste buds. You'll really start to taste all the fresh fruit and veggies. While your green juice should be sustaining your appetite for longer periods by this point, I often find it comforting to chew something during lunch. If I have extra fruits or veggies at lunch, I skip having them with my snack.

**1 glass of lemon water
(12 ounces/355ml)**

Your bowels should be much happier now, moving either at night after your big raw dinner or first thing in the morning. It is still always a good idea to drink a big glass of water upon rising for immediate hydration.

**1 cup of green tea
(8 ounces/235ml)**

Green tea is optional, so if you are not experiencing any caffeine headaches, feel free to skip it.

**1 glass of New Year Morning Green Juice
(16 ounces/475ml)
(see recipe on page 39)**

By now, you are hopefully really enjoying and looking forward to your green juice each morning. I really love the flavor profile of this recipe. If cilantro is not your thing, don't include it. Also, if the juice starts to taste too sweet, just reduce the amount of pineapple.

Swiss chard has been ranked by the World's Healthiest Foods Organization as the second-most nutrient-rich vegetable in the world (after spinach). Most Swiss chard has a bit of red coloring, so it may stain your juicer or turn your juice a faint brown.

Optional lunch addition:
1 cup (120g) of carrot sticks. *Have this if you're still hungry or low-energy after your juice.*

INGREDIENTS

1 large carrot or 2 small carrots, top and bottom removed

4 to 5 celery stalks, bottoms removed

3 to 4 Swiss chard leaves

¼ lemon, peeled, remainder reserved for morning lemon water (optional)

chard-carrot green
JUICE

1 Wash the carrot, celery, and chard leaves.

2 Run all ingredients through your juicer, scrape off foam (if desired), and enjoy!

SUPERFOOD HIGHLIGHT: swiss chard

Swiss chard is one of those wonderful super greens full of antioxidants, including kaempferol, a phytonutrient that is also found in broccoli and kale. There is research showing that kaempferol may have the potential to assist in fighting cancer. Swiss chard is also a cousin to the beet family, and it contains phytonutrients found in beets called betalains, which have been shown to provide antioxidant, anti-inflammatory, and detoxification support. Baby Swiss chard is a great addition to salads, as it mixes well with other super greens like baby spinach and watercress. To prepare Swiss chard, just rinse before running it through your juicer, stems and all.

spicy winter green
JUICE

Sometimes in the midst of the winter cold, a little spice can be a big pick-me-up. I've found that the winter blues are no match for a hot kick of cayenne in my green juice—it wakes up my taste buds and offers a jolt to my body and mind.

INGREDIENTS

3 to 4 celery stalks, bottoms removed

Big handful of spinach (⅔ bunch)

⅛ pineapple or ¾ cup (125g) pineapple chunks

⅛ tsp sea salt

Pinch of cayenne pepper (⅛ tsp or less)

1 Wash the celery and spinach.

2 Top and tail the pineapple, peel it, and cut into pieces that will fit through your juicer.

3 Run the vegetables and pineapple through your juicer and scrape off foam (if desired).

4 Season with salt and cayenne, and enjoy!

avocado tomato
DELIGHT

When I travel, I always try to hit a grocery store when I get to my destination city, and I purchase two items without fail: an avocado and a tomato. With these, I can make a meal. When I am not eating raw, I'll add them to whole-grain bread for a sandwich. When I am, I enjoy them all on their own with a touch of sea salt and a drizzle of extra-virgin olive oil. Heavenly!

INGREDIENTS

1 ripe tomato, thinly sliced

1 avocado, thinly sliced

Sea salt, to taste

Extra-virgin olive oil, for drizzling

1 Arrange tomato and avocado slices on a plate.

2 Sprinkle with salt to taste and drizzle with olive oil.

Who said you can't have spaghetti on a cleanse? Making spaghetti out of raw zucchini is super easy with a spiralizer, a very inexpensive tool that makes raw cooking a lot more fun. I highly recommend purchasing one, and then try this recipe, which will really satiate you.

INGREDIENTS

5 to 6 ripe tomatoes, cut into chunks

¼ white onion, cut into chunks

2 garlic cloves

Handful of basil (6 to 7 leaves)

1 to 2 stems fresh oregano

1 to 2 tbsp extra-virgin olive oil

Sea salt and pepper, to taste

1 to 2 small zucchinis

raw zucchini
SPAGHETTI

1 To create a fantastic raw marinara, in a high-speed blender or Vitamix, combine tomatoes, onion, garlic gloves, basil, oregano, and olive oil. Pulse until smooth, then add salt and pepper to taste.

2 If you have one, use a spiralizer to create spaghetti-like curls out of the zucchinis. If you don't have one, just shred the zucchini with a carrot peeler, peeling and all, or finely chop into small sticks.

3 Arrange the zucchini "spaghetti" in a bowl and top with the marinara sauce.

DAY

4

Today is your day. You should feel fully energized and totally comfortable with this new way of eating. My hope is that, as you return gradually to your former eating habits, you will take with you several of your new habits, the most important of which is drinking a green juice every morning.

**1 glass of lemon water
(12 ounces/355ml)**

Your bowels should be running like clockwork now, allowing you to fully absorb the nutrients from all the wonderful fruits and vegetables you're consuming. Keep up your water habit first thing in the morning—not just during a cleanse, but for every single day of your life.

**1 cup of green tea
(8 ounces/235ml)**

Still optional. If you don't need the caffeine, skip it.

**1 glass of New Year Morning Green Juice (16 ounces/475ml)
(see recipe on page 39)**

Did you wake up craving your morning greens? You should notice a definite change in your "green palate" since the first day of your cleanse. If your Morning Green Juice tastes too sweet, that means you have succeeded in cleansing your body of the toxins that lead to sweet cravings. Good for you! If you continue to drink a green juice every morning, you can use less and less fruit and move toward a purely green juice (no fruit included). Try cutting the pineapple in half today.

Today is the day to let go of the fruit and start making your green juice as green as can be. Cabbage is related to the broccoli family, and in addition to containing high quantities of vitamin C and other antioxidants, it contains a variety of nutrients that promote overall stomach and intestinal health.

Optional lunch addition:
1 cup (100g) of sliced cucumbers and celery sticks (add sea salt to taste). *Have this if you're still hungry after the juice.*

INGREDIENTS

2 to 3 green cabbage leaves

3 to 5 celery stalks, bottoms removed

1 cucumber

Handful of parsley leaves (from 3 to 4 stems)

¼ lemon, peeled (optional)

cabbage green
JUICE

1 Wash the cabbage, celery, cucumber, and parsley.

2 If you need to cut the greenness, use ¼ lemon. If not, skip it.

3 Run all ingredients through your juicer, scrape off foam (if desired), and enjoy!

SUPERFOOD HIGHLIGHT:
freshwater blue-green algae

Composed of almost 70 percent protein, blue-green algae also offers dozens upon dozens of vitamins and minerals as well as essential fatty acids. In particular, it's loaded with all the crucial B vitamins, which help improve brain function, stabilize moods, and generate red blood cells for improved vitality—among their many other wonderful benefits. E3Live is a wonderful source, harvesting and drying the algae naturally to preserve its nutrients.

blue-green algae
JUICE
(aka happy juice)

Freshwater blue-green algae (Aphanizomenon flos-aquae, or AFA) is an ancient, nutrient-packed plant sold in powder form at natural food stores. When I add it to my juice, it increases my energy and boosts my mood, so I call this drink "happy juice."

Optional snack addition: 1 cup (110g) of carrot and celery sticks. *Nosh on these veggies if your snack juice doesn't satiate you.*

INGREDIENTS

1 cucumber

3 to 5 celery stalks, bottoms removed

3 to 4 kale leaves

½ lemon, peeled (optional)

1 to 2 tsp blue-green algae (E3Live AFA brand recommended)

1 Wash the cucumber, celery, and kale.

2 If you need to cut the greenness, use ½ lemon. If not, skip it.

3 Run all vegetables and lemon through your juicer and scrape off foam (if desired).

4 Add the algae, and enjoy!

Time for some tasty raw soup. I highly recommend using a Vitamix; however, a high-speed blender will work too. By this point in your cleanse, you might want a little something warm in your tummy, so I definitely recommend the extra step of heating this up a bit on the stove. Food is still considered raw as long as it is not heated above 115°F (50°C). Above this temperature, the vegetables start losing nutrients to the heat.

raw cauliflower SOUP

INGREDIENTS

¼ cup (35g) pine nuts

1 cup (235ml) water

½ head of cauliflower, cut up into florets

1 garlic clove

¼ sweet or white onion

1 to 2 tsp Italian spice

2 to 3 tsp extra-virgin olive oil

Sea salt and pepper, to taste

Parsley leaves, to garnish

1 Place the pine nuts and water in the Vitamix or high-speed blender, and run on High for a minute or two to create a creamy base.

2 Add the cauliflower florets, garlic, and onion. Blend until the texture is smooth.

3 Add the Italian spice and olive oil, and season with salt and pepper to taste.

4 Blend on High until smooth, adding more water as needed until it reaches desired consistency.

5 If you would like a warm soup while keeping it raw, pour it into a saucepan on the stove and heat over the lowest possible temperature. Stir constantly until the soup is warm to the touch, and remove immediately. Ladle into a bowl and garnish with parsley and black cracked pepper.

This salad is so simple and delicious. I often use it as a base for more complicated salads, as it contains such great building blocks. However, it's also great just as it is.

simple winter SALAD

INGREDIENTS

1 head of butter lettuce, torn or chopped

1 medium carrot, shredded

½ cucumber, peeled and thinly sliced

2 to 3 green (spring) onions, thinly sliced

Handful of watercress (½ bunch), stems removed (optional)

1 tbsp whole-grain mustard

1 tbsp raw apple cider vinegar

2 tbsp extra-virgin olive oil

Sea salt and pepper, to taste

Pinch of cayenne

1 Combine the butter lettuce, shredded carrot, cucumber slices, and green onions in a large salad bowl. Add watercress, if using, and toss well.

2 To make the dressing, whisk together the mustard, apple cider vinegar, and olive oil in a separate bowl. Season with salt and pepper to taste, add a pinch of cayenne, and whisk to combine.

3 Sprinkle salt onto the salad, pour dressing over the top, and toss gently.

CONGRATS! You have successfully completed your New Year 4-Day Cleanse. Your intestines, body, and mind should be thanking you now. You should be feeling more energized than ever. In addition, you might notice that you have more mental clarity and even a nice glow to your skin. For information and recipes that will help you maintain the wonderful benefits of your cleanse and help you transition to post-cleanse eating, please turn to page 149.

CHAPTER 3

spring
4-DAY
GREEN JUICE
& RAW FOOD
CLEANSE

Spring is one of the most popular seasons to begin a cleanse. Why? Well, there's a reason they call it spring cleaning! After all, a winter spent indulging in comfort food and cozying up in warm sweaters would make anyone lethargic and desperate for an energy boost.

If you're too busy to make all the juices yourself at home for this cleanse, you can substitute any of our cold-pressed juices sold in stores for the homemade recipes in this chapter. You can find the store locations closest to you on our website (www.drinkdailygreens.com).

To make everything easier, we have provided a shopping list (on the pages that follow) and broken it up by juice ingredients and raw food ingredients (which you will need for your dinner each night). If you plan to buy ready-to-drink Daily Greens juices for your cleanse, simply skip directly to the food shopping list.

Not sure where to shop? I love shopping locally and supporting local farmers, so I highly recommend hitting your farmers market to see if you can find the majority of your list there. You will most likely also need to make a quick trip to the grocery store. Happy shopping!

juice shopping list

VEGETABLES	QUANTITY
Bok choy	1 head
Carrot	5 medium
Celery	2 heads
Collard greens (or Swiss chard)	1 bunch
Cucumber	10 medium
Ginger root	¼-inch (0.6 cm) piece
Kale	2 bunches
Romaine (cos)	1 head
Spinach	4 bunches or 2 large boxes, prewashed

FRUIT	QUANTITY
Fuji apple	1 medium
Lemon	2 medium
Lime	1 small
Pear	6 medium
Pineapple	1 whole
Strawberry	1 pint

HERBS	QUANTITY
Basil	1 bunch
Cilantro	1 bunch
Mint	1 bunch
Parsley	1 bunch

OTHER	QUANTITY
Vanilla extract	1 small vial

food shopping list

VEGETABLES	QUANTITY
Arugula (rocket)	1 box, prewashed
Avocado	2 medium
Bok choy	1 head
Carrot	1 medium
Celery	1 stalk
Chinese cabbage*	1 head
Collard greens (or cos)	1 bunch
Cucumber	1 medium
Endive (curly endive)	1 head
Fennel	1 bulb
Garlic	1 clove
Ginger root	½-inch (1.3 cm) piece
Green (spring) onion	1 bunch
Radish	7–9 small
Red cabbage	1 head
Red bell pepper (red capsicum)	1 medium
Shallots	1 bulb
Super greens	1 box, prewashed
Watercress	1 bunch

FRUIT	QUANTITY
Blood orange	1 medium
Fuji apple	1 medium
Pomegranate	1 whole

HERBS	QUANTITY
Basil	1 bunch
Mint	1 bunch
Parsley	1 bunch
Tarragon	1 bunch

NUTS/SEEDS	QUANTITY
Almonds (chopped, raw)	¼ cup (38g)
Almond slivers (raw)	¼ cup (30g)
Pine nuts (raw)	1 tbsp
Sesame seeds (black)	1 tbsp
Walnuts (halved, raw)	2 tbsp

OTHER	QUANTITY
Apple cider vinegar (Bragg's)	1 small container
Cayenne pepper	small amount of dried powder
Coconut nectar (raw)	1 small container
Coconut vinegar (raw)	1 small container
Green tea	4 individual servings
Kimchi* (raw)	1 medium jar
Maple syrup	1 small container
Miso paste (raw, white)	1 small container
Mustard (whole-grain)	1 small container
Olive oil (extra-virgin)	1 small container
Pepper (black, cracked)	1 grinder of whole seeds
Sea salt (pink Himalayan)	1 shaker of whole crystals
Soy sauce (nama shoyu)	1 small container

*If you plan to purchase premade kimchi, there is no need to also purchase Chinese cabbage to make your own kimchi.

DAY

1

Congratulations on starting your Spring 4-Day Cleanse! This is the beginning of a whole new you. It's spring outside, and now it's time to do your own internal spring cleaning! Throughout your cleanse, in addition to consuming the various juices and raw foods presented here, be sure to drink plenty of water over the course of each day to stay hydrated.

BREAKFAST

1 glass of lemon water (12 ounces/355ml)

Upon rising, drink a big glass of water with a squeeze of lemon. If you don't mind it, I suggest heating it up a bit. Lemon will help your digestive tract start moving. This will be especially important during the first couple days of your cleanse as you drop your morning coffee.

1 cup of green tea (8 ounces/235ml)

Next, enjoy a hot cup of green tea. The warmth from the tea will also help start moving your digestive tract along, and if you are experiencing caffeine withdrawal, the tea will help quell your headache. Green tea is also full of antioxidants.

spring morning green
JUICE

D
G

Finally, my favorite part of the morning: preparing my Morning Green Juice. As you can probably tell by now, this morning juice is an essential part of my day. And it can be an essential part of yours too! If you prefer to try your own recipe, keep it simple and follow my "Simple Green Juice Formula" (see page 21).

INGREDIENTS

1 cucumber

Big handful of spinach (⅔ bunch)

1 pear

Handful of basil (3 to 4 leaves)

1 Wash the cucumber, spinach, pear, and basil.

2 Cut and core the pear and cut into pieces that will fit through your juicer.

3 Run all ingredients through your juicer, scrape off foam (if desired), and enjoy!

pineapple-mint green
JUICE

I always love the combination of pineapple and mint. Mint in particular really wakes up my taste buds: It's so aromatic and adds a refreshing kick to any green juice.

Optional lunch addition: 1 Fuji apple, sliced. *On the first day in particular, you may be hungry. If your green juice does not satiate you, enjoy this cut-up fruit afterward.*

INGREDIENTS

1 cucumber

Big handful of spinach (⅔ bunch)

½ Fuji apple

Handful of mint (3 to 4 leaves)

⅛ pineapple or ¾ cup (125g) pineapple chunks

1 Wash the cucumber, spinach, apple, and mint.

2 Cut and core the apple and cut into pieces that will fit in your juicer.

3 Top and tail the pineapple, peel it, and cut into pieces that will fit through your juicer.

4 Run all ingredients through your juicer, scrape off foam (if desired), and enjoy!

sweet greens
JUICE
with ginger

Fresh ginger root is wonderful in vegetable stir-fry dishes, and it adds a touch of spice to any green juice or smoothie. You can find it year-round in the produce section of your local market.

Optional snack addition:
1 pear, sliced. *Snack on the fruit if you are not feeling satiated from your mid-afternoon green juice.*

INGREDIENTS

½ Fuji apple

½ pear

5 kale leaves

5 celery stalks, bottoms removed

¼-inch (0.6 cm) piece ginger root

¼ lemon, peeled, remainder reserved for morning lemon water (optional)

1 Wash the apple, pear, kale, celery, and ginger.

2 Cut and core the apple and pear, and cut into pieces that will fit through your juicer.

3 Run all ingredients through your juicer, scrape off foam (if desired), and enjoy!

These finger-food cups offer a unique and delicious sweet-savory flavor combination. I adore blood oranges. They are incredibly beautiful and so different from regular oranges. Endive is such an interesting and mild green, and here it also functions as a fun, ready-made appetizer cup.

INGREDIENTS

1 head of endive (curly endive)

1 blood orange (or regular orange, if you can't find a blood orange)

2 tbsp raw apple cider vinegar

½ cup (90g) pomegranate seeds

1 tbsp raw pine nuts

blood orange & pomegranate
ENDIVE CUPS

1 Remove individual endive leaves and arrange them in a star-shaped circle on a plate.

2 Peel and slice the orange, making sure to remove the membrane. Squeeze the remaining juice from the membrane into a separate dish and combine with an equal amount of apple cider vinegar to form the dressing.

3 Place the orange slices on the open endive leaves, then sprinkle pomegranate seeds and pine nuts on top.

4 Drizzle the dressing over each endive cup, and enjoy!

red cabbage & walnut
SALAD

This fun and hearty salad came about as I was preparing for a hamburger cookout. I needed something to complement all the burgers and pickles, and this salad was an instant hit.

INGREDIENTS

½ head of red cabbage, thinly sliced

1 to 2 green (spring) onions, thinly sliced

3 tbsp extra-virgin olive oil

2 tbsp whole-grain mustard

2 tbsp raw apple cider vinegar

Sea salt and pepper, to taste

2 tbsp raw halved walnuts

Maple syrup, for drizzling

1 Combine the cabbage and green onions in a large salad bowl.

2 To make the vinaigrette, whisk together the olive oil, mustard, and apple cider vinegar in a separate bowl, and season with salt and pepper to taste.

3 Pour the vinaigrette over the cabbage mixture and toss well.

4 Top with walnuts, drizzle with maple syrup, and serve!

DAY 2

Day 2 has arrived. I know that yesterday was tough, but today will be better. Your energy will begin to pick up, and you will feel less hungry. This is a sign that your intestines are starting to more fully absorb the nutrients from all the raw fruit and veggies in your green juice and your raw food dinner.

1 glass of lemon water (12 ounces/355ml)

Like yesterday, when you rise, have a glass of water, preferably heated, with a squeeze of lemon in it. If your bowels did not move yesterday, hopefully this will get things moving.

1 cup of green tea (8 ounces/235ml)

Your need for caffeine should be a bit less today as you start to gain energy from your green juice.

1 glass of Spring Morning Green Juice (16 ounces/475ml) (see page 67)

Today should be an easier experience with the juicer—hopefully you're getting the hang of it. To help develop your "green palate," I find it best to stick with the same simple green juice each morning.

carrot-pineapple green
JUICE

D
—
G

Carrots make a great substitute for fruit in a green juice, adding sweetness and loads of vitamin A, which promotes good eyesight.

Optional lunch addition: 1 cup (165g) chopped pineapple. *Your need for additional fruit should lessen each day of the cleanse. However, if your blood sugar is running low, have this fruit after your juice.*

INGREDIENTS

1 cucumber

2 carrots, tops and bottoms removed

3 celery stalks, bottoms removed

4 to 5 kale leaves

⅛ pineapple or ¾ cup (125g) pineapple chunks

1 Wash the cucumber, carrots, celery, and kale.

2 Top and tail the pineapple, peel it, and cut into pieces that will fit through your juicer.

3 Run all ingredients through your juicer, scrape off foam (if desired), and enjoy!

strawberry green
JUICE

Strawberries are chock-full of vitamin C and many other essential nutrients and antioxidants. For parents out there, this green juice comes kid-tested, as my son Cooper loves it.

Optional snack addition: 1 cup (110g) of strawberries. *Only consume more fruit with your green juice snack if you feel hungry or low on energy.*

INGREDIENTS

5 strawberries

Big handful of spinach (⅔ bunch)

4 romaine (cos) leaves

½ apple

Handful of mint (3 to 4 leaves)

⅛ pineapple or ¾ cup (125g) pineapple chunks

1 Wash the strawberries, spinach, romaine, apple, and mint.

2 Cut and core the apple and cut into pieces that will fit through your juicer.

3 Top and tail the pineapple, peel it, and cut into pieces that will fit through your juicer.

4 Run all ingredients through your juicer, scrape off foam (if desired) and enjoy!

collard green
WRAPS

Collard greens are a wonderful alternative to romaine leaves for the purpose of making wraps, but they are thicker and stiffer so you need a tiny bit of steam to make them pliable. To prepare, just wash and use the entire leaf.

INGREDIENTS

4 collard green (or cos) leaves

2 tbsp raw miso paste

1 medium carrot, thinly sliced or shredded

½ red bell pepper (red capsicum), thinly sliced

1 celery stalk, thinly sliced or shredded

¼ cucumber, finely chopped

1 avocado, thinly sliced

1 large basil leaf, torn into bits (or several small ones)

1 Wash the collard green leaves, then steam them ever so slightly by dipping them very briefly in boiling water, approximately one minute. (If you're using romaine [cos], don't steam.) This cook time should be just long enough to make them pliable for forming wraps, but not long enough to lose nutrients to the heat.

2 Coat each leaf with ½ tablespoon miso paste.

3 Distribute carrot, red pepper, celery, and cucumber evenly onto each leaf.

4 Top each leaf with avocado slices, and sprinkle with torn basil.

5 To eat, wrap the sides of each leaf inward to cover the filling, and enjoy!

My dear chef friend, Mike New-house—also godfather to my son Cooper—inspired this salad while we were visiting in Boze-man, Montana, one spring. Mike prepared this beautiful spread of chopped fennel, apple, cu-cumbers, and torn mint drizzled with some wonderful balsamic reduction that he and his wife, Meta, had brought back from their travels in Italy. The aromatic properties of the mint and fennel combined with the crispness of the apples and cucumbers made me immediately forget that it was freezing cold outside. When I got back home, I immediately created a hearty salad out of these ingredients, combining them with super greens. Super greens are a mix of greens such as watercress, chard, baby kale, mâche, arugula, spinach, and tatsoi, to name a few.

INGREDIENTS

½ Fuji apple, thinly sliced

½ fennel bulb, thinly sliced

½ cucumber, thinly sliced

Handful of mint (6 to 7 leaves), chopped

Bowl of super greens (spinach, kale, arugula [rocket], watercress [stems removed], Swiss chard, mâche, and tatsoi)

2 tbsp raw coconut vinegar

3 tbsp extra-virgin olive oil

Sea salt and pepper, to taste

super greens & mint
SALAD

1 Combine the sliced apple, fennel, cucumber, and chopped mint in a bowl and toss gently.

2 Transfer the mixture to a large bowl with super greens such as spinach, kale, arugula, water-cress, Swiss chard, mâche, and tatsoi. Toss well to combine.

3 To make the dressing, whisk together the coconut vinegar and olive oil in a separate bowl.

4 Pour the dressing over the salad and toss gently. Season with salt and pepper to taste, and serve!

⏱ TIME SAVER

Most grocery stores now carry prewashed packages of super greens.

DAY
3

Welcome to Day 3 of your cleanse. You should really have the hang of things now. You should also start to experience increased mental clarity as your body continues to eliminate toxins. Your intestines should be getting into more of a rhythm, as you develop new habits. By Day 3, you might also start noticing an awakening of your taste buds. You'll really start to taste all the fresh fruits and veggies. While your green juice should be sustaining your appetite for longer periods by this point, I often find it comforting to chew something during lunch. If I have extra fruits or veggies at lunch, I skip having them with my snack.

BREAKFAST

1 glass of lemon water (12 ounces/355ml)

Your bowels should be much happier now, moving either at night after your big raw dinner or first thing in the morning. It is still always a good idea to drink a big glass of water upon rising for immediate hydration.

1 cup of green tea (8 ounces/235ml)

Green tea is optional, so if you are not experiencing any caffeine headaches, feel free to skip it.

1 glass of Spring Morning Green Juice (16 ounces/475ml) (see recipe on page 67)

By now, you are hopefully really enjoying and looking forward to your green juice each morning. If the juice starts to taste too sweet, just reduce the amount of pear.

pear-vanilla green
JUICE

Vanilla adds a note of sweetness to this green juice without adding calories.

💧 **Optional lunch addition:**
1 sliced pear. *Have this only if you're still hungry or low on energy after your lunch juice.*

INGREDIENTS

1 pear

1 cucumber

Big handful of spinach (⅔ bunch)

Handful of cilantro (coriander) leaves (from 3 to 4 stems) (optional, but recommended)

¼ lime, peeled

2 tsp vanilla extract

1 Wash the pear, cucumber, spinach, and cilantro.

2 Cut and core the pear and cut into pieces that will fit in your juicer.

3 Run all ingredients except vanilla through your juicer and scrape off foam (if desired).

4 Add the vanilla extract, stir, and enjoy!

Carrots have many wonderful nutrients, but like fruit, they contain a lot of natural sugar. Thanks to their sweetness, they are a great substitute for fruit in a green juice—but be careful not to add too many. I love this recipe's combination of carrots and cilantro.

 Optional snack addition:
1 cup (120g) of carrot sticks. *Again, if you don't need extra veggies after your mid-afternoon juice, skip this.*

INGREDIENTS

4 to 5 small carrots, tops and bottoms removed

1 cucumber

4 to 5 kale leaves

Handful of cilantro (coriander) leaves (from 3 to 4 stems) (optional, but recommended)

¼ lime, peeled

carrot-cilantro green
JUICE

D / G

1 Wash the carrots, cucumber, kale, and cilantro.

2 Cut the long stems off the cilantro leaves.

3 Run all ingredients through your juicer, and scrape off foam (if desired).

mixed radish
SLICES

Radishes are one of the first spring veggies to make an appearance at the farmers market. Take advantage of this early-spring crop by sampling the different varieties available, including the gorgeous watermelon varietal. Enjoy these herby finger-food appetizers while you prepare your salad.

INGREDIENTS

5 to 6 radishes (all types), sliced paper-thin

Extra-virgin olive oil, for drizzling

Handful of parsley leaves (from 5 to 6 stems), chopped

Handful of basil (6 to 7 leaves), chopped

Sea salt, to taste

1 Arrange radish slices on a plate and drizzle with olive oil.

2 Sprinkle with chopped parsley and basil, then season with salt to taste.

watercress arugula
SALAD

I love the combination of these two super greens. They are both a touch spicy, and make for a party in your mouth. To me, this salad tastes like spring in a bowl.

INGREDIENTS

2 cups (40g) baby arugula (rocket)

2 cups (70g) watercress, stems removed

Handful of tarragon (from 2 to 3 stems), chopped

3 tbsp extra-virgin olive oil

2 tbsp raw apple cider vinegar

1 tbsp thinly chopped shallots

Sea salt and pepper, to taste

2 to 3 radishes, thinly sliced

¼ cup (25g) chopped raw almonds

1 Combine arugula and watercress in a large salad bowl and toss well. Add tarragon and toss again.

2 To make the dressing, whisk together the olive oil, apple cider vinegar, and shallots in a separate bowl. Add salt and pepper to taste.

3 Pour dressing over the greens, add radishes and almonds, and toss gently. Enjoy!

DAY 4

Today is your day. You should feel fully energized and totally comfortable with this new way of eating. My hope is that, as you return gradually to your former eating habits, you will take with you several of your new habits, the most important of which is drinking a green juice every morning.

1 glass of lemon water
(12 ounces/355ml)

Your bowels should be running like clock-work now, allowing you to fully absorb the nutrients from all the wonderful fruits and vegetables you're consuming. Keep up your water habit first thing in the morning—not just during a cleanse, but for every single day of your life.

1 cup of green tea
(8 ounces/235ml)

Still optional. If you don't need the caffeine, skip it.

1 glass of Spring Morning Green Juice
(16 ounces/475ml)
(see recipe on page 67)

Did you wake up craving your morning greens? You should notice a definite change in your "green palate" since the first day of your cleanse. If your Morning Green Juice tastes too sweet, that means you have succeeded in cleansing your body of the toxins that lead to sweet cravings. Good for you! If you continue to drink a green juice every morning, you can use less and less fruit and move toward a purely green juice (no fruit included). Try cutting the pear in half today.

super green
JUICE

D / G

Today is the day to let go of the fruit and start making your green juice as green as can be. This juice contains an amazing superfood—collard greens.

Optional lunch addition: 1 cup (90–120g) of chopped veggies (such as carrots, cucumbers, and celery). *If your juice isn't enough, nosh on some veggies today instead of fruit.*

INGREDIENTS

1 cucumber

3 celery stalks, bottoms removed

3 romaine (cos) leaves

2 collard green (or Swiss chard) leaves

Handful of parsley leaves (from 3 to 4 stems)

½ lemon, peeled (optional)

1 Wash the cucumber, celery, romaine, collard green leaves, and parsley.

2 If you need to cut the greenness, use ½ lemon. If not, skip it.

3 Run all ingredients through your juicer, scrape off foam (if desired), and enjoy!

bok choy green
JUICE

Bok choy is another veggie that makes an early appearance at the spring farmers market. Look for firm, bright green leaves without any browning or small holes.

INGREDIENTS

1 cucumber

1 head of bok choy

Big handful of spinach (⅔ bunch)

Handful of basil (3 to 4 leaves)

½ lemon, peeled (optional)

1 Wash the cucumber, bok choy, spinach, and basil.

2 If you need to cut the greenness, use ½ lemon. If not, skip it.

3 Run all ingredients through your juicer, scrape off foam (if desired), and enjoy!

raw kimchi

Kimchi is a combination of flavorful Korean-style fermented vegetables. It's a wonderful raw food option: The fermentation process softens the texture of nutrient-rich vegetables (making them easier to chew and digest) without cooking away the nutrients. Fermentation also produces probiotic bacteria, which is important for your overall immune system and digestive health. For a hearty appetizer, combine your kimchi with raw almond slivers or peanuts.

INGREDIENTS

½ head of cabbage (preferably Chinese cabbage), cored and chopped into bite-size pieces

½ cup (145g) sea salt

2 small green (spring) onions, thinly sliced

½ garlic clove, minced

1 tbsp raw coconut nectar

¼-inch (0.6 cm) piece ginger root, minced

½ tbsp cayenne pepper (or less, if too spicy)

1 Place the chopped cabbage in a large bowl and add the salt. Toss to combine.

2 Transfer to a large zip-tight plastic bag and remove excess air. Leave the bag at room temperature for at least six hours or overnight.

3 Drain the excess liquid from the cabbage.

4 Combine the remaining ingredients in a large bowl. Add the cabbage and toss well, coating it completely with the onion mixture.

5 Transfer to an airtight mason jar and leave at room temperature for four days.

6 After four days, carefully open the jar to let the gas escape. Prepare to serve, or store in the fridge.

⏱ TIME SAVER

While it's fun to make kimchi yourself, it is also very time consuming. Thankfully, most supermarkets and natural-food stores carry several great raw kimchi brands. My personal favorites are made by Oh-Kimchi. Look for them in the refrigerated section next to the tofu.

Bok choy is very satiating, especially when I'm craving Asian food. Plus, it is one of the easiest greens to prepare as it requires minimal trimming.

raw bok choy
SALAD

INGREDIENTS

½ head of bok choy, roughly chopped

2 to 3 green (spring) onions, thinly sliced

1 small avocado, diced

¼ cup (30g) raw almond slivers

1 tbsp black sesame seeds

3 tbsp extra-virgin olive oil

1½ tbsp coconut vinegar

1 tbsp raw soy sauce (nama shoyu)

3 tbsp maple syrup

¼-inch (0.6 cm) piece ginger root, minced

½ garlic clove, minced

1 Arrange bok choy on a platter. Add green onions, avocado, almonds, and sesame seeds.

2 To make the dressing, whisk together the olive oil, coconut vinegar, soy sauce, maple syrup, ginger, and garlic.

3 Drizzle over bok choy platter and serve.

CONGRATS! You have successfully completed your Spring 4-Day Green Juice and Raw Food Cleanse. Your intestines, body, and mind should be thanking you now. You should be feeling more energized than ever. In addition, you might notice that you have more mental clarity and even a nice glow to your skin. For information and recipes that will help you maintain the wonderful benefits of your cleanse and help you transition to post-cleanse eating, please turn to page 149.

CHAPTER 4

summer
4-DAY GREEN JUICE & RAW FOOD CLEANSE

Summer might seem like an odd time to cleanse since we're naturally more active in this season, but barbecues and trips to the beach can mean a big increase in the consumption of animal proteins—and a big drop in your energy levels! So if you've got an upcoming vacation or wedding that you'd like to look and feel your best for, the 4-day cleanse is the best way to jump-start your progress. If you're too busy to make all the juices yourself at home, you can substitute any of our cold-pressed juices sold in stores for the homemade recipes in this chapter. Our website (www.drinkdailygreens.com) can give you the closest store locations.

To make everything easier, we have provided a shopping list (on the pages that follow) and broken it up by juice ingredients and raw food ingredients (which you will need for your dinner each night). If you plan to buy ready-to-drink Daily Greens juices for your cleanse, simply skip directly to the food shopping list.

Not sure where to shop? I love shopping locally and supporting local farmers, so I highly recommend hitting your farmers market to see if you can find the majority of your list there. You will most likely also need to make a quick trip to the grocery store. Happy shopping!

juice shopping list

VEGETABLES	QUANTITY
Celery	2 heads
Collard greens (or kale)	1 small bunch
Cucumber	9 medium
Dandelion greens	1 bunch
Ginger root	¼-inch (0.6 cm) piece
Kale	1 small bunch
Spinach	4 bunches or 2 large boxes, prewashed
Watercress	1 bunch
Yellow bell pepper (yellow capsicum)	1 medium
Zucchini	3 medium

FRUIT	QUANTITY
Cantaloupe	½ melon
Green grapes	1 bunch
Honeydew	½ melon
Lemon	2 medium
Peach	1 medium
Pear	1 medium
Pineapple	¾ cup (125g) chunks
Watermelon	1 small melon

HERBS	QUANTITY
Basil	1 bunch
Cilantro (coriander)	1 bunch
Mint	1 bunch

NUTS/SEEDS	QUANTITY
Chia seeds (white)	¼ cup (40g)

OTHER	QUANTITY
Sea salt (pink Himalayan)	1 shaker of whole crystals

food shopping list

VEGETABLES	QUANTITY
Avocado	6 small
Carrots	1 bag carrot sticks
Celery	2 stalks
Cherry tomato	1 pint
Cucumber	2 medium
Garlic	1 bulb
Green cabbage	1 head
Green (spring) onion	1 bunch
Jalapeño	1 small
Kale	1 bunch
Purple cabbage	1 head
Red onion	1 small
Red bell pepper (red capsicum)	1–2 medium
Roma tomato	2 medium
Romaine (cos)	2 heads of hearts
Super greens	1 box, prewashed
Tomato	4–5 medium
White onion	1 small
Yellow bell pepper (yellow capsicum)	2–3 medium

FRUIT	QUANTITY
Lemon	1 medium
Lime	1 small
Watermelon	½ small melon

HERBS	QUANTITY
Basil	1 bunch
Cilantro (coriander)	½ bunch
Mint	½ bunch
Parsley	1 bunch

NUTS/SEEDS	QUANTITY
Almond slivers (raw)	½ cup (60g)
Cashews or pine nuts (raw)	½ cup (75g)

OTHER	QUANTITY
Almond oil	1 small container
Apple cider vinegar (Bragg's)	1 small container
Cayenne pepper	small amount of dried powder
Coconut nectar (raw)	1 small container
Green tea	4 individual servings
Mustard (whole-grain)	1 small container
Nutritional yeast	small amount of dried powder
Olive oil (extra-virgin)	1 small container
Pepper (black, cracked)	1 grinder of whole seeds
Sea salt (pink Himalayan)	1 shaker of whole crystals
White vinegar	1 small container

DAY 1

Congratulations on starting your Summer 4-Day Cleanse. This is the beginning of a whole new you. You're off your normal routine during the summertime, and this is a great time to do a quick cleanse to reset your mind and body. Throughout your cleanse, in addition to consuming the various juices and raw foods presented here, be sure to drink plenty of water over the course of each day to stay hydrated.

**1 glass of lemon water
(12 ounces/355ml)**

Upon rising, drink a big glass of water with a squeeze of lemon. If you don't mind it, I suggest heating it up a bit. Lemon will help your digestive tract start moving. This will be especially important during the first couple days of your cleanse as you drop your morning coffee.

**1 cup of green tea
(8 ounces/235ml)**

Next, enjoy a hot cup of green tea. The warmth from the tea will also help start moving your digestive tract along, and if you are having caffeine withdrawal, this will help quell your headache. Green tea is also full of antioxidants.

summer morning green
JUICE

D / G

Finally, my favorite part of the morning: preparing my Morning Green Juice. This morning juice is an essential part of my day. And it can be an essential part of yours too! If you prefer to try your own recipe, keep it simple and follow my "Simple Green Juice Formula" (see page 21).

INGREDIENTS

1 cucumber

1 to 2 collard green (or kale) leaves

Handful of mint (3 to 4 leaves)

1½ cups (230g) watermelon chunks

1 Wash the cucumber, collard green leaves, and mint.

2 Run all ingredients through your juicer, scrape off foam (if desired), and enjoy!

Several years ago, my sister turned me onto the benefit of consuming chia seeds for hydration. She would put them in a mason jar with water, a little lime, and Stevia to soak overnight. She would drink it the next morning after her run, to rehydrate and replenish. I tried it a few times and liked it so much that I started soaking the chia seeds overnight in filtered water and then adding them to my green juice the next day. Soaking chia seeds releases all of their fabulous nutrients—including super-hydrating electrolyte minerals, which will make your green juice more hydrating than ever. They also give your green juice an interesting texture.

Optional lunch addition:
1 small bowl of cubed watermelon and cantaloupe (add salt to bring out the sweetness). *If your green juice does not satiate you, enjoy this cut-up fruit afterward.*

INGREDIENTS

1 cucumber

Big handful of spinach (⅔ bunch)

Handful of mint (3 to 4 leaves) (optional)

½ cup (80g) cubed cantaloupe

½ cup (80g) cubed watermelon

⅛ tsp sea salt

¼ cup (40g) chia seeds, soaked overnight in filtered water, then drained (optional)

melon green
JUICE
with chia seeds

1 Wash the cucumber, spinach, and mint.

2 Run all ingredients except salt and seeds through your juicer and scrape off foam (if desired).

3 Sprinkle in the salt and chia seeds (if using), stir, and enjoy!

SUPERFOOD HIGHLIGHT:
chia seeds

Chia seeds are a true superfood. The ancient Mayans and Aztecs of Mexico used them for energy; in fact, "chia" is the Mayan word for "strength." Packed with soluble fiber and those ultra-healthy omega-3 fats, these whole-grain seeds are also rich in protein and calcium. Chia seeds are also wonderful in ground form, which can be added to a green smoothie or sprinkled on top of a raw salad. You'll find them in dried form at your local health-food store, and when kept dry, they can be stored for long periods of time (read: years!).

sweet honeydew green
JUICE

Honeydew is one of my favorite summertime fruits. Related to watermelon and cantaloupe (but better!), it simply melts in your mouth. It really sweetens up a green juice so nicely.

Optional snack addition: ½ cup (90g) of cubed honeydew melon. *Snack on the fruit if you are not feeling satiated from your mid-afternoon green juice.*

INGREDIENTS

1 cucumber

Big handful of spinach (⅔ bunch)

½ cup (75g) seedless green grapes

½ cup (90g) cubed honeydew melon

1 Wash the cucumber, spinach, and grapes.

2 Run all ingredients through your juicer, scrape off foam (if desired), and enjoy.

Nothing makes me happier in the summer than fresh guacamole. When I am doing a cleanse, I simply substitute raw crisp veggies for corn chips to get the same satisfying experience.

INGREDIENTS

guacamole

2 avocados, cubed

2 roma tomatoes, chopped

¼ red onion, finely chopped

1 to 2 garlic cloves, minced

½ jalapeño, seeded and minced

½ bunch of cilantro (coriander), leaves only, chopped

Juice of ½ lime

Sea salt and pepper, to taste

Dash of cayenne pepper (optional)

veggies for dipping

½ cup (60g) carrot sticks

½ cup (50g) celery sticks

½ cup (45g) sliced red bell pepper (red capsicum)

raw guacamole & veggies

D
G

1 Combine avocado, tomatoes, onion, garlic, and jalapeño in a small bowl. Stir with a fork until the avocado is chunky.

2 Add cilantro and lime juice, then season with salt and pepper to taste.

3 If you like spice, add a dash of cayenne and mix well into the guacamole.

4 Dip the carrots, celery, and red peppers in the guacamole, and enjoy!

🕐 TIME SAVER

Most grocery stores now carry premade fresh guacamole that will save you the time of making it on your own. Be sure that it is freshly made and not something in a vacuum-sealed package, which will not be fresh or necessarily raw.

cherry tomato & avocado
SALAD

This is such a simple salad, but it really hits the spot on a hot summer day. I love anything that combines my two favorite veggies: avocado and tomatoes.

INGREDIENTS

Bowl of super greens (spinach, kale, arugula [rocket], watercress (stems removed), Swiss chard, mâche, and tatsoi)

½ cup (75g) cherry tomatoes, halved

1 small avocado, cubed

2 tbsp extra-virgin olive oil

2 tbsp raw apple cider vinegar

Sea salt and pepper, to taste

1 Combine super greens with tomatoes and avocado in a large bowl.

2 To make the dressing, whisk together the olive oil and apple cider vinegar in a separate bowl, then season with salt and pepper to taste.

3 Pour the dressing over the salad and toss gently.

⏱ TIME SAVER

To skim a few minutes off your prep time, most grocery stores carry containers of prewashed super greens.

DAY 2

Day 2 has arrived. I know that yesterday was tough, but today will be better. Your energy will begin to pick up and you will feel less hungry. This is a sign that your intestines are starting to more fully absorb the nutrients from all the raw fruit and veggies in your green juice and your raw food dinner.

BREAKFAST

1 glass of lemon water
(12 ounces/355ml)

Like yesterday, when you rise, have a glass of water, preferably heated, with a squeeze of lemon in it. If your bowels did not move yesterday, hopefully this will get things moving.

1 cup of green tea
(8 ounces/235ml)

Your need for caffeine should be a bit less today as you start to gain energy from your green juice.

1 glass of Summer Morning
Green Juice
(16 ounces/475ml)
(see page 95)

Today should be an easier experience with the juicer—hopefully you're getting the hang of it. To help develop your "green palate," I find it best to stick with the same simple green juice each morning.

Peaches may be my all-time favorite fruit during the summer. I love stopping at farm stands and buying them directly from farmers. Don't refrigerate them, as they taste much better warm and ripe straight from the farm. They make a scrumptious addition to a green juice.

💧 **Optional lunch addition:**

1 peach, sliced. *Your need for additional fruit should decrease each day of the cleanse. However, you don't want to run out of energy, so if your energy or blood sugar is running low, have this sliced fruit after your juice.*

INGREDIENTS

1 cucumber

1 peach

Big handful of spinach (⅔ bunch)

Handful of mint (3 to 4 leaves)

¼-inch (0.6 cm) piece ginger root

⅛ pineapple or ¾ cup (125g) pineapple chunks

peach green
JUICE

1 Wash the cucumber, peach, spinach, mint, and ginger.

2 Cut and core the peach, and cut into pieces that will fit through your juicer.

3 Top and tail the pineapple, peel it, and cut into pieces that will fit through your juicer.

4 Run all ingredients through your juicer, scrape off foam (if desired), and enjoy!

SUPERFOOD HIGHLIGHT:
ginger root

Ginger root has been used for centuries to alleviate symptoms of gastrointestinal upset and as an aid for digestion. Recently, ginger has been shown in studies to help prevent and ease symptoms of motion sickness, including nausea, vomiting, and dizziness. It can be easily stored, unsealed, in the crisper drawer of your refrigerator for long periods of time.

Zucchini makes a perfect substitute for cucumber in any green juice. It gives the juice a slightly creamy texture. I love using zucchini in my green juice all summer long while it's in season.

Optional snack addition:
1 pear, sliced. *Only eat this fruit if you still feel hungry or low on energy after your green juice snack.*

INGREDIENTS

1 pear

1 zucchini

Big handful of spinach (⅔ bunch)

Handful of cilantro (coriander) leaves (from 3 to 4 stems)

zucchini-pear green JUICE
with cilantro

1 Wash all ingredients well.

2 Cut and core the pear, and cut into pieces that will fit through your juicer.

3 Chop the zucchini into pieces that will fit through your juicer.

4 Run all ingredients through your juicer, scrape off foam (if desired), and enjoy!

SUPERFOOD HIGHLIGHT:
cilantro

Some people absolutely love cilantro. Others report that it tastes like soap. If you are in the "soap" category, just skip it in lieu of another dark leafy herb. However, if you are one of the lucky folks who find the smell "intoxicating," use it often in green juices or smoothies or tossed into your favorite salad. Cilantro offers loads of antioxidants, phytonutrients, and minerals such as calcium and potassium. You'll also get vitamins A, C, and K and even some B vitamins from this potent herb. It's truly a cleansing and healing dynamo that's fantastic during a juice cleanse. To store cilantro, loosely wrap the stems in a paper towel to keep it free of moisture. Put it in a plastic bag and store in the fridge to preserve it for a longer period of time. Stored properly, it can last up to three days. When juicing, cut off the long stems, as they can be bitter.

watermelon cucumber
SALAD

D/G

I was inspired to create this salad one Fourth of July. The secret to the success is the sea salt, which brings out the sweetness in the watermelon and cucumbers.

INGREDIENTS

1 cucumber, peeled and cubed

Sea salt, to taste

2 cups (300g) chopped watermelon

Handful of mint (6 to 7 leaves)

Handful of basil (6 to 7 leaves)

1 Place the cucumber into a salad bowl and sprinkle a light layer of salt over the top.

2 Add the watermelon and sprinkle another light layer of salt on top.

3 Tear up pieces of mint and basil and sprinkle over the salad. Toss gently, and enjoy.

This is a crowd favorite among my friends and family. Living in Texas, I get invited to more than my share of BBQs. Since my diet is 100 percent plant-based, this presents a challenge for me. I often volunteer to bring a dish that will complement the standard BBQ fare. Coleslaw always seems to fit the bill, but Southern-style coleslaw is usually drowning in a creamy mayonnaise dressing. So, I came up with my own healthy version that is 100 percent raw and plant-based. The result is a hearty blend of familiar coleslaw ingredients that will really fill you up.

INGREDIENTS

¼ head of purple cabbage, thinly sliced

¼ head of green cabbage, thinly sliced

½ yellow pepper (yellow capsicum), finely chopped

2 to 3 green (spring) onions, thinly sliced

1 small avocado, chopped

1 tbsp raw almond oil

¼ cup (30g) raw almond slivers

Sea salt, to taste

summer
COLESLAW

1 Combine the cabbages, pepper, and green onions in a salad bowl and toss to mix well.

2 Add the avocado, almond oil, and almond slivers and toss gently until the mixture is coated with avocado.

3 Season with salt to taste, and serve!

DAY 3

Welcome to Day 3 of your cleanse. You should really have the hang of things now. You should also start to experience increased mental clarity as your body continues to eliminate toxins. Your intestines should be getting into more of a rhythm, as you develop new habits. By Day 3, you might also start noticing an awakening of your taste buds. You'll really start to taste all the fresh fruit and veggies. While your green juice should be sustaining your appetite for longer periods by this point, I often find it comforting to chew something during lunch. If I have extra fruits or veggies at lunch, I skip having them with my snack.

**1 glass of lemon water
(12 ounces/355ml)**

Your bowels should be much happier now, moving either at night after your big raw dinner or first thing in the morning. It is still always a good idea to drink a big glass of water upon rising for immediate hydration.

**1 cup of green tea
(8 ounces/235ml)**

Green tea is optional, so if you are not experiencing any caffeine headaches, feel free to skip it.

**1 glass of Summer Morning
Green Juice
(16 ounces/475ml)
(see recipe on page 95)**

By now, you are hopefully really enjoying and looking forward to your green juice each morning. If mint is not your thing, don't include it. Also, if the juice starts to taste too sweet, reduce the amount of watermelon.

Cantaloupe and zucchini actually come from the same plant family, so they combine well in a green juice. They both grow from vines that crawl across the ground. In my mom's garden growing up, I loved hunting for and picking them.

 Optional lunch addition: 1 cup (160g) of chopped cantaloupe. *Eat this only if you're still hungry or low on energy after your lunch juice.*

INGREDIENTS

1 zucchini

Big handful of spinach (approximately ⅔ bunch)

Handful of basil (3 to 4 leaves)

1 cup (160g) cubed cantaloupe

¼ lemon, peeled, remainder reserved for morning lemon water

Sea salt, to taste

zucchini-cantaloupe green
JUICE

D / G

1 Wash the zucchini, spinach, and basil.

2 Run all ingredients except salt through your juicer and scrape off foam (if desired).

3 Sprinkle in a dash of salt, stir, and enjoy.

SUPERFOOD HIGHLIGHT:
spinach

Spinach is one of the most nutrient-dense foods in existence. A single cup is a great source of calcium and iron, and it contains far more vitamin K than the daily allowance, as well as high doses of vitamin A and magnesium. Spinach, unlike most other dark leafy greens, is actually pretty neutral from a flavor perspective. As a result, it makes a fantastic base for a green juice or green smoothie. Baby spinach is also a wonderful addition to any salad.

Do not wash spinach before storing, as the exposure to water encourages spoilage. Place spinach in a plastic storage bag and wrap the bag tightly around the spinach, squeezing out as much of the air as possible. Store in the refrigerator, where it will keep fresh for up to five days.

honeydew-watercress green
JUICE

This green juice combines three of my favorite summer ingredients: sweet honeydew, creamy zucchini, and a touch of spiciness from the watercress.

Optional snack addition:
1 cup (180g) of cubed honeydew melon. *If you don't feel the need for extra fruit after your juice snack, skip it.*

INGREDIENTS

1 zucchini

Handful of watercress (⅓ bunch)

Handful of cilantro (coriander) leaves (from 3 to 4 stems)

3 to 4 celery stalks, bottoms removed

1 cup (180g) cubed honeydew melon

⅛ tsp sea salt (optional, but recommended)

1 Wash the zucchini, watercress, cilantro, and celery.

2 Run all ingredients through your juicer and scrape off foam (if desired).

3 Season with salt, if desired, stir, and enjoy!

gazpacho

One of my favorite summer treats is freshly made raw gazpacho. I love grabbing all the ingredients from a summer farmers market and blending up a big batch to enjoy over the course of several days. It hardly takes any time to prepare, and it's even better the next day—stored in an airtight container in the refrigerator overnight.

INGREDIENTS

1 yellow bell pepper (yellow capsicum)

Handful of basil (6 to 7 leaves)

½ jalapeño, seeded

1 cucumber, peeled and cut into large chunks

1 white (sweet) onion, cut into quarters

2 garlic cloves

1 cup (235ml) water

2 tbsp extra-virgin olive oil

2 tbsp white vinegar

4 to 5 ripe tomatoes, cut in halves or quarters

Sea salt and pepper, to taste

1 Combine all ingredients except tomatoes in a high-speed blender or Vitamix and blend on chopped setting.

2 Add tomatoes and pulse until desired consistency.

3 Season with salt and pepper to taste.

I love the flavor profile of Caesar salad, but I missed out on it for years until I figured out a substitute for the dressing.

vegan caesar SALAD

INGREDIENTS

4 to 5 heart of romaine (cos) leaves, roughly chopped

Handful of parsley leaves (from 5 to 6 stems), chopped

½ cup (75g) raw cashew nuts or pine nuts (I prefer pine nuts)

2 tbsp lemon juice

½ tsp raw coconut nectar

3 tbsp nutritional yeast flakes

1 to 2 garlic cloves

½ tsp sea salt, or more, to taste

½ tsp pepper, or more, to taste

1 Combine the romaine and parsley in a salad bowl and toss.

2 To make the dressing, combine all remaining ingredients in your high-speed blender or Vita-mix, and blend on High.

3 Pour the dressing over the chopped romaine and toss to mix well.

⏱ TIME SAVER

Several natural-food brands now make ready-to-go vegan Caesar dressings that I always keep in my fridge. My personal favorite is from Follow Your Heart.

DAY 4

Today is your day. You should feel fully energized and be totally comfortable with this new way of eating. My hope is that, as you return gradually to your former eating habits, you will take with you several of your new habits, the most important of which is drinking a green juice every morning.

BREAKFAST

**1 glass of lemon water
(12 ounces/355ml)**

Your bowels should be running like clockwork now, allowing you to fully absorb the nutrients from all the wonderful fruits and vegetables you're consuming. Keep up your water habit first thing in the morning—not just during a cleanse, but every single day of your life.

**1 cup of green tea
(8 ounces/235ml)**

Still optional. If you don't need the caffeine, skip it.

**1 glass of Summer Morning
Green Juice (16 ounces/475ml)
(see recipe on page 95)**

Did you wake up craving your morning greens? You should notice a definite change in your "green palate" since the first day of your cleanse. If your Morning Green Juice tastes too sweet, that means you have succeeded in cleansing your body of the toxins that lead to sweet cravings. Good for you! If you continue to drink a green juice every morning, you can use less and less fruit and move toward a purely green juice (no fruit included). Try cutting the watermelon in half today.

yellow bell pepper
JUICE

Don't let the color of this drink fool you. It's chock-full of green goodness!

Optional lunch addition:
1 cup (90g) of sliced yellow bell pepper (yellow capsicum). *If your juice isn't enough, nosh on this as well.*

INGREDIENTS

1 cucumber

3 to 5 celery stalks, bottoms removed

2 to 3 kale leaves

1 yellow bell pepper (yellow capsicum)

Handful of basil (3 to 4 leaves)

½ lemon, peeled (optional)

1 Wash the cucumber, celery, kale, bell pepper, and basil.

2 Remove the top and seeds from the bell pepper and cut into pieces that will fit through your juicer.

3 If you need to cut the "greenness," use ½ lemon. If not, skip it.

4 Run all ingredients through your juicer, scrape off foam (if desired), and enjoy!

You can buy dandelion greens at your local health-food store. Never pick them from your yard! Pesticides are used abundantly on lawns, and even if you don't use pesticides on your lawn, your neighbors most likely do on theirs, and these pesticides will find their way onto the weeds. Store dandelion greens in an airtight bag in the refrigerator. Do not wash them before storing, as contact with water can facilitate spoilage. When you are ready to use them, wash them well and throw them into your juicer, stems and all.

◐ **Optional snack addition:**
1 cup (90–120g) of chopped veggies (such as carrots, cucumbers, and celery). *Snack on these veggies only if your mid-afternoon juice doesn't satiate you.*

INGREDIENTS

1 cucumber

3 celery stalks, bottoms removed

Big handful of spinach (⅔ bunch)

Handful of dandelion greens (5 to 6 stems)

Handful of basil (3 to 4 leaves)

½ lemon, peeled (optional)

dandelion green
JUICE

1 Wash the cucumber, celery, spinach, dandelion greens, and basil.

2 If you need to cut the greenness, use ½ lemon. If not, skip it.

3 Run all ingredients through your juicer, scrape off foam (if desired), and enjoy!

SUPERFOOD HIGHLIGHT:
dandelion greens

Who knew that these would be one of the best things to throw into your juicer? Dandelion greens have some powerful health benefits, as they are packed with nutrients that support the body's ability to detoxify, fight allergies, and normalize blood sugar. Cultivated in the wild, dandelion greens are high in vitamins A, B1, B2, and B6, as well as magnesium; they are also packed with iron, potassium, and calcium. Dandelions are one of the most potent greens in assisting with rehabilitation and detoxification of the liver.

Kale is often not very palatable in salads, but adding a bit of salt and lemon will soften it up and break it down to a friendlier texture. The secret to this salad, however, is the avocado, which forms a nice creamy coat on the kale.

INGREDIENTS

5 to 6 kale leaves (1 bunch), torn into bite-size pieces

2 to 3 green (spring) onions, thinly sliced

1 yellow or red bell pepper (capsicum), finely chopped

Handful of parsley leaves (from 5 to 6 stems), finely chopped

2 tbsp lemon juice

2 tbsp almond oil

⅛ tsp cayenne pepper

Sea salt and pepper, to taste

1 avocado, chopped

¼ cup (30g) raw almond slivers, for garnish

raw kale SALAD

1 Combine the kale, green onions, bell pepper, and parsley in a large bowl and toss.

2 To make the dressing, whisk together the lemon juice, almond oil, and cayenne in a separate bowl. Season with salt and pepper to taste.

3 Pour dressing over the salad and toss gently.

4 Add avocado to the bowl, and massage into the kale leaves to form a creamy dressing from the mixture. Wash your hands after massaging to remove any cayenne pepper.

5 Sprinkle with almond slivers and enjoy!

These wraps are super basic and very easy to assemble. Romaine wraps are my go-to meal when I don't have time to prepare a more sophisticated salad. These contain all the flavors of a salad, but without all the chopping and tossing.

INGREDIENTS

5 heart of romaine (cos) leaves

2 tbsp whole-grain mustard

1 avocado, sliced

1 medium carrot, thinly sliced or shredded

romaine lettuce
WRAPS

1 Arrange the romaine leaves on a plate and spread a small amount of mustard on each leaf.

2 Distribute avocado and carrot evenly onto each leaf.

3 To eat, wrap the sides of each leaf inward to cover the filling, and enjoy!

CONGRATS! You have successfully completed your Summer 4-Day Green Juice and Raw Food Cleanse. Your intestines, body, and mind should be thanking you now. You should be feeling more energized than ever. In addition, you might notice that you have more mental clarity and even a nice glow to your skin. For information and recipes that will help you maintain the wonderful benefits of your cleanse and help you transition to post-cleanse eating, please turn to page 149.

CHAPTER 5

fall

4-DAY GREEN JUICE & RAW FOOD CLEANSE

The wonderful flavors of fall make this season an incredible time to cleanse. Succulent butternut squash, creamy pumpkin, and flavorful zucchini—delicious! Plus fall cleansing is a fantastic way to get healthy and focused before the upcoming holiday season.

If you're too busy to make all the juices yourself at home, you can substitute any of our cold-pressed juices sold in stores for the homemade recipes in this chapter. Our website (www.drinkdailygreens.com) can give you the closest store locations.

To make everything easier, we have provided a shopping list (on the pages that follow) and broken it up by juice ingredients and raw food ingredients (which you will need for your dinner each night). If you plan to buy ready-to-drink Daily Greens juices for your cleanse, simply skip directly to the food shopping list.

Not sure where to shop? I love shopping locally and supporting local farmers, so I highly recommend hitting your farmers market to see if you can find the majority of your list there. You will most likely also need to make a quick trip to the grocery store. Happy shopping!

VEGETABLES	QUANTITY
Broccoli	½ stalk (florets removed)
Carrot	2 medium
Celery	4 heads
Cucumber	4 medium
Fennel	½ bulb
Ginger	¼-inch (0.6 cm) piece
Kale	3 bunches
Jalapeño	1 small
Red bell pepper (red capsicum)	1 medium
Romaine (cos)	2 heads
Spinach	1½ bunches or 2 small boxes, prewashed
Zucchini	1 medium

FRUIT	QUANTITY
Apple	5 medium
Granny Smith apple	1 medium
Green grapes (seedless)	½ bunch
Lemon	3 medium
Orange	1 medium
Pineapple	½ whole

HERBS	QUANTITY
Basil	1 bunch
Parsley	1 bunch

OTHER	QUANTITY
Sea salt (pink Himalayan)	1 shaker of whole crystals
Turmeric powder	dash of dried powder

food shopping list

VEGETABLES	QUANTITY
Avocado	7 medium
Butternut squash	½ small
Carrot	4 medium
Celery	2 stalks
Cherry tomato	1 pint
Fennel	½ bulb
Garlic	3–5 cloves
Ginger	¼-inch (0.6 cm) piece
Jalapeño	1 small
Mixed baby greens	2 boxes, prewashed
Red bell pepper (red capsicum)	1 medium
Red onion	1 small
Romaine (cos)	2 heads of hearts
Roma tomato	6 medium
Sprouts	1 small container
White onion	1 small

FRUIT	QUANTITY
Lemon	1 medium
Lime	2 small

HERBS	QUANTITY
Basil	1 bunch
Cilantro (coriander)	1 bunch
Mint	1 bunch
Parsley	1 bunch
Rosemary	1 bunch
Tarragon	1 bunch

NUTS/SEEDS	QUANTITY
Almonds (chopped, raw)	1 tbsp
Hempseed (raw)	2 tbsp
Pine nuts (raw)	¼ cup (35g)
Pistachios (raw hulled)	1 tbsp
Pumpkin seeds (raw)	2–3 tbsp

OTHER	QUANTITY
Agave nectar (raw)	1 small container
Almond oil	1 small container
Cayenne pepper	dash of dried powder (optional)
Crackers (raw)	1 package
Cranberries (dried)	1 handful (for garnish)
Currants (dried)	1 tbsp
Green tea	4 individual servings
Maple syrup	1 small container
Olive oil (extra-virgin)	1 small container
Pepper (black, cracked)	1 grinder of whole seeds
Sea salt (pink Himalayan)	1 shaker of whole crystals

DAY

1

Congratulations on starting your Fall 4-Day Cleanse. This is the beginning of a whole new you. With the crispness of fall in the air, it's time to settle into your normal routines and de-tox your body from all that summer fun and overindulgence. Throughout your cleanse, in addition to consuming the various juices and raw foods presented here, be sure to drink plenty of water over the course of each day to stay hydrated.

BREAKFAST

**1 glass of lemon water
(12 ounces/355ml)**

Upon rising, drink a big glass of water with a squeeze of lemon. If you don't mind it, I suggest heating it up a bit. Lemon will help your digestive tract start moving. This will be especially important during the first couple days of your cleanse as you drop your morning coffee.

**1 cup of green tea
(8 ounces/235ml)**

Next, enjoy a hot cup of green tea. The warmth from the tea will also help start moving your digestive tract along, and if you are having caffeine withdrawal, this will help quell your headache. Green tea is also full of antioxidants.

fall morning green
JUICE

D/G

Finally, my favorite part of the morning: preparing my Morning Green Juice. As you can probably tell by now, I have a serious love affair with my Morning Green Juice. Now it is time to start your own love affair! If you prefer to try your own recipe, keep it simple and follow my "Simple Green Juice Formula" (see page 21).

INGREDIENTS

5 to 6 celery stalks, bottoms removed

4 to 5 kale leaves

1 apple

Handful of parsley leaves (from 3 to 4 stems)

1 Wash the celery, kale, apple, and parsley.

2 Cut and core the apple, and cut into pieces that will fit through your juicer.

3 Run all ingredients through your juicer, scrape off foam (if desired), and enjoy!

This is a great beginner green juice. It doesn't contain any dark leafy greens, so it technically does not follow the "Simple Green Juice Formula." However, it's a terrific way to ease into green juice and it makes a satisfying first-day lunch.

Optional lunch addition:
1 cup (165g) of pineapple chunks. *On the first day in particular, you may be hungry. If your green juice does not satiate you, enjoy this cut-up fruit as part of your lunch.*

INGREDIENTS

1 cucumber

4 to 5 celery stalks, bottoms removed

2 to 3 romaine (cos) leaves

¼ pineapple or 1½ cups (250g) pineapple chunks

¼ lemon, peeled, remainder reserved for morning lemon water

pineapple with greens
JUICE

1 Wash the cucumber, celery, and romaine.

2 Top and tail the pineapple, peel it, and cut into pieces that will fit through your juicer.

3 Run all ingredients through your juicer, scrape off foam (if desired), and enjoy!

Fennel is one of my favorite ingredients to add to both salads and green juice. Although related to carrots, dill, parsley, and coriander, fennel has such a distinct taste (kind of like licorice) that it adds a big punch of flavor to your juice.

 Optional snack addition:

1 apple, sliced. *Only snack on the fruit if you are not feeling satiated from your mid-afternoon green juice.*

INGREDIENTS

4 to 5 celery stalks, bottoms removed

4 to 5 kale leaves

1 apple

¼ fennel bulb

¼ lemon, peeled

fennel-apple green
JUICE

D / G

1 Wash the celery, kale, apple, and fennel.

2 Cut and core the apple, and cut into pieces that will fit through your juicer.

3 Run all ingredients through your juicer, scrape off foam (if desired), and enjoy.

SUPERFOOD HIGHLIGHT:
fennel

Fennel is rich in vitamin C, which helps boost the immune system, and it also contains potassium, calcium, iron, manganese, copper, phosphorus, and folate. Another bonus? You can eat the whole vegetable, from its white or light-green bulb to its stalks and fluffy green fronds. I tend to use the bulb for salads and the whole thing for juicing. Fennel is in season from fall through spring and can be found at your local natural-food store. When shopping for fennel, look for bulbs that are clean, firm, and solid. Store fresh fennel in your refrigerator's crisper, where it should keep fresh for about four days.

When I step into fall, I get the urge to make soup. However, most soups cook down vegetables to the point where there are not many nutrients left. I learned about raw soups many years ago and became hooked. The basic concept of a raw soup is to use your high-speed blender, or preferably a Vitamix, to pulverize your veggies until they reach a smooth soup-like texture. If you really feel like you need a little warmth, you can heat the soup a bit on the stove without cooking away all the nutrients. The raw food temperature limit is 115°F (50°C). When your food spends any time above this temperature, it will start to lose nutrients at a rapid rate.

INGREDIENTS

2 medium carrots, roughly chopped

½ red bell pepper (red capsicum), seeded and roughly chopped

¼-inch (0.6 cm) piece ginger root

Handful of parsley leaves (from 5 to 6 stems)

1 avocado

½ to 1 cup (120 to 235ml) water

Sea salt and pepper, to taste

Extra-virgin olive oil, for drizzling

raw carrot
SOUP

1 Wash the carrots, bell pepper, ginger, and parsley.

2 Place the carrots, bell pepper, ginger, half of parsley, and avocado meat in a high-speed blender or Vitamix.

3 Blend on High until smooth, adding water as needed until it reaches desired consistency.

4 Season with salt and pepper to taste.

5 If you would like a warm soup while keeping it raw, pour it into a saucepan on the stove and heat over the lowest possible temperature. Stir constantly until the soup is warm to the touch, and remove immediately. Ladle into a bowl, drizzle with olive oil, and garnish with remaining parsley leaves.

fall fennel
SALAD

This is one of my favorite salads as the summer fades into cooler weather. I have been making this salad for years for my friends and family, and I seem to make it a bit differently each time depending on what herbs and nuts I have on hand. The taste can change dramatically if you alter the combinations, so feel free to experiment and find the blend of herbs and nuts that best suits your taste.

INGREDIENTS

Bowl of mixed baby greens (such as baby red and green romaine [cos])

½ fennel bulb, finely sliced

½ cup (75g) cherry tomatoes, halved

Handful of tarragon (2 to 3 stems), finely chopped

Handful of basil (6 to 7 leaves), finely chopped

¼ cup (35g) pine nuts

2 tsp lemon juice (juice of ½ lemon)

2 tsp almond oil

Sea salt and pepper, to taste

½ avocado or 1 small avocado, thinly sliced

1 Combine the mixed greens, fennel, tomatoes, tarragon, and basil in a large bowl. Toss gently.

2 Add the pine nuts, lemon juice, and almond oil, and toss to combine.

3 Season with salt and pepper to taste.

4 Layer the sliced avocado over the top of the salad, and enjoy!

⏱ TIME SAVER

If you're trying to save time, most grocery stores now carry containers of prewashed mixed baby greens. My favorite brand is Organic Girls.

DAY 2

Day 2 has arrived. I know that yesterday was tough, but today will be better. Your energy will begin to pick up and you will feel less hungry. This is a sign that your intestines are starting to more fully absorb the nutrients from all the raw fruit and veggies in your green juice and your raw food dinner.

**1 glass of lemon water
(12 ounces/355ml)**

Like yesterday, when you rise, have a glass of water, preferably heated, with a squeeze of lemon in it. If your bowels did not move yesterday, hopefully this will get things moving.

**1 cup of green tea
(8 ounces/235ml)**

Your need for caffeine should be a bit less today, as you start to gain energy from your green juice.

**1 glass of Fall Morning
Green Juice (16 ounces/475ml)
(see recipe on page 123)**

Today should be an easier experience with the juicer—hopefully you're getting the hang of it. To help develop your "green palate," I find it best to stick with the same simple green juice each morning.

orange-carrot
JUICE
with greens

While I usually stick to juice recipes that are green in color, drinking your carrots is highly beneficial.

Optional lunch addition:
1 orange, quartered. *Your need for additional fruit should lessen each day, but eat this fruit if your blood sugar is low.*

INGREDIENTS

2 medium carrots, tops and bottoms removed

1 cucumber

Small handful of spinach (½ bunch)

⅛ pineapple or ¾ cup (125g) pineapple chunks

½ orange, peeled

¼ lemon, peeled, remainder reserved for morning lemon water

Dash of turmeric powder (½ tsp or less)

1 Wash the carrots, cucumber, and spinach.

2 Top and tail the pineapple, peel it, and cut into pieces that will fit through your juicer.

3 Run all ingredients except turmeric through your juicer and scrape off foam (if desired).

4 Add turmeric, stir, and enjoy!

When shopping for kale, you might see a few different varieties, including curly kale, ornamental kale, and dinosaur kale. You can use them all for juicing, but I recommend dinosaur kale, as it usually results in the most juice.

 Optional snack addition:
1 small bowl of grapes (no more than 10). *Again, only eat this fruit with your green juice snack if you feel hungry or low on energy.*

INGREDIENTS

1 cup (150g) seedless green grapes

5 to 6 kale leaves

2 to 3 romaine (cos) leaves

¼-inch (0.6 cm) piece ginger root

¼ lemon, peeled

kale-grape green
JUICE

1 Wash the grapes, kale, romaine, and ginger.

2 Run all ingredients through your juicer, scrape off foam (if desired), and enjoy.

SUPERFOOD HIGHLIGHT:
kale

While kale has received a ton of hype, it's actually well deserved. Kale contains high quantities of powerful antioxidants, such as vitamins A and C, and it's loaded with vitamin K. It's a good source of vitamins B1, B2, and B6, as well as the all-important electrolyte minerals sodium, potassium, calcium, and magnesium. Kale also has the potential to help reduce the risk of cancer, and its effects have recently been shown to reach five forms of cancer: bladder, breast, colon, ovary, and prostate. It's also a detoxing dynamo, helping the body to clear out toxins. Store your kale in an airtight plastic bag in the refrigerator for up to five days. Don't wash kale before storing. When you're ready for juicing, simply wash and use the entire leaf. However, if you're making a delicate salad, use only the leaves and either discard the stems or save them for juicing.

raw salsa & veggies

Raw salsa is easy to make in a high-speed blender or a Vitamix. Once you have the basics down, try adding interesting ingredients, like pineapple, or substituting tomatillos for the roma tomatoes.

INGREDIENTS

salsa

½ white (sweet) onion, roughly chopped

¼ bunch of cilantro (coriander), leaves only

1 to 2 garlic cloves

½ jalapeño, seeded and roughly chopped

4 roma tomatoes, quartered

Juice of ½ lime

Sea salt and pepper, to taste

veggies for dipping

½ cup (60g) carrot sticks

½ cup (50g) celery sticks

½ cup (45g) sliced red bell pepper (red capsicum)

1 Combine the onion, cilantro, garlic, and jalapeño in a high-speed blender or Vitamix, and run on high until minced.

2 Add tomatoes and lime juice and pulse until it reaches desired consistency.

3 Season with salt and pepper to taste.

4 Dip the carrots, celery, and red peppers in the salsa, and enjoy!

⏱ TIME SAVER

Many grocery stores now carry premade raw salsas. Be sure the label says "fresh" and "raw," as most salsas are cooked or include cooked ingredients.

These tacos are so fun and should hit the spot for Tex-Mex night. A Texas staple, guacamole is also a wonderful raw, vegan dip. It works perfectly as the filling in a romaine lettuce wrap.

INGREDIENTS

guacamole

2 avocados, chopped

2 roma tomatoes, chopped

¼ red onion, finely chopped

1 to 2 garlic cloves, finely chopped

½ jalapeño, seeds removed and finely chopped

½ bunch of cilantro (coriander), leaves only, chopped

Juice of ½ lime

Sea salt and pepper, to taste

Dash of cayenne pepper (optional)

tacos

4 to 5 heart of romaine (cos) leaves

2 to 3 tbsp raw pumpkin seeds

1 cup (50g) sprouts (any kind)

raw guacamole TACOS

1 Combine avocado, tomatoes, onion, garlic, and jalapeño in a small bowl. Stir with a fork until the avocado is chunky.

2 Add the cilantro and lime juice, then season with salt and pepper to taste.

3 If you like spice, add a dash of cayenne and mix well into the guacamole.

4 Arrange the romaine leaves on a plate, and add a scoop of guacamole on each leaf. Top with pumpkin seeds and sprouts.

5 To eat, fold up the sides of the leaf like a taco, and enjoy.

⏱ TIME SAVER

Most grocery stores now carry premade fresh guacamole that will save you the time of making it on your own. Be sure that it is freshly made and not something in a vacuum-sealed package, which will not be fresh or necessarily raw.

DAY 3

Welcome to Day 3 of your cleanse. You should really have the hang of things now. You should also start to experience increased mental clarity as your body continues to eliminate toxins. Your intestines should be getting into more of a rhythm, as you develop new habits. By Day 3, you might also start noticing an awakening of your taste buds. You'll really start to taste all the fresh fruit and veggies. While your green juice should be sustaining your appetite for longer periods by this point, I often find it comforting to chew something during lunch. If I have extra fruits or veggies at lunch, I skip having them with my snack.

BREAKFAST

**1 glass of lemon water
(12 ounces/355ml)**

Your bowels should be much happier now, moving either at night after your big raw dinner or first thing in the morning. It is still always a good idea to drink a big glass of water upon rising for immediate hydration.

**1 cup of green tea
(8 ounces/235ml)**

Green tea is optional, so if you are not experiencing any caffeine headaches, feel free to skip it.

**1 glass of Fall Morning
Green Juice (16 ounces/475ml)
(see recipe on page 123)**

By now, you are hopefully really enjoying and looking forward to your green juice each morning. I really love the simplicity of this recipe. While any apple will work, try using a Fuji apple. It's a bit crisper, while not too sweet. But, if the juice does start to taste too sweet, try reducing the amount of apple.

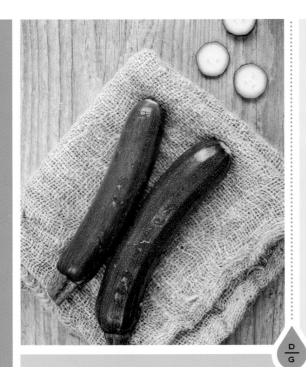

kale-zucchini green
JUICE

D/G

Zucchini is a wonderful substitute for cucumber in a green juice, and it adds a nice creamy texture. While it is technically a summer vegetable, it usually peaks late in the season and can often be found at early-fall farmers markets.

Optional lunch addition:
1 Granny Smith apple, sliced. *Only eat this fruit if you are still hungry or low on energy after your lunch juice.*

INGREDIENTS

1 zucchini

4 to 5 kale leaves

1 Granny Smith apple

¼ lemon, peeled, remainder reserved for morning lemon water (optional)

1 Wash the zucchini, kale, and apple.

2 Cut and core the apple and cut into pieces that will fit through the juicer.

3 Run all ingredients through your juicer, scrape off foam (if desired), and enjoy!

Jalapeños have so many fantastic nutrients, including high doses of vitamin C. In fact, one small jalapeño provides a day's worth of vitamin C. Adding a bit of jalapeño to a green juice really mixes things up and adds a fun new dimension.

◖ **Optional snack addition:** 1 to 2 cups (135 to 270g) chopped cucumber (add sea salt for flavor). *If you're not still hungry after your mid-afternoon juice, skip this.*

INGREDIENTS

½ cucumber

3 to 4 celery stalks, bottoms removed

4 to 5 kale leaves

¼ jalapeño or more if desired, seeded (optional, but recommended)

⅛ pineapple or ¾ cup (125g) pineapple chunks

⅛ tsp sea salt (optional, but recommended)

pineapple-jalapeño green
JUICE

D
G

1 Wash the cucumber, celery, kale, and jalapeño.

2 Top and tail the pineapple, peel it, and cut into pieces that will fit through your juicer.

3 Run all ingredients except jalapeño through your juicer.

4 Add ¼ portion of jalapeño and taste to check spice level. If more spice is needed, add more jalapeño a little at a time until the desired spiciness is obtained.

5 Scrape off foam and sprinkle with sea salt (if desired), stir, and enjoy!

avocado
CUP

My husband, Kirk, made up this little gem. Although he definitely prefers grilling to any other form of food preparation, he sometimes comes up with some ingenious raw dishes. This is so simple and takes only seconds to prepare, yet it is extremely satisfying.

INGREDIENTS

½ avocado (pit removed)

1 tbsp raw hulled pistachios

Almond oil (or other nut oil), for drizzling

Sea salt, to taste

1 Sprinkle avocado with pistachios, then drizzle with almond oil.

2 Season with salt to taste and enjoy!

heavenly herb
SALAD

This salad is one of my all-time favorites—it's like a comfort food. The mixture of avocado and almonds makes it hearty and filling. But for me, the essence of a salad is in its herbs, and this one has all three of my favorites: mint, basil, and cilantro. One of my dear chef friends, John Cain, requests that I make this salad for him frequently. It is so fun to watch him eat it, as he makes cute happy noises the entire time. I think that he, too, is completely seduced by the heavenly combination of herbs.

INGREDIENTS

Bowl of mixed baby greens (such as red and green romaine [cos])

Handful of mint (6 to 7 leaves), finely chopped

Handful of basil (6 to 7 leaves), finely chopped

Handful of cilantro (coriander) leaves (from 5 to 6 stems), finely chopped

1 small avocado or ½ large avocado, diced

1 tbsp dried currants

1 tbsp roughly chopped almonds

1 tbsp almond oil

1 tsp agave nectar

Juice of ½ lime

Sea salt, to taste

1 Combine the mixed greens, mint, basil, and cilantro in a salad bowl and toss.

2 Add the avocado, currants, almonds, almond oil, agave nectar, and lime juice, and toss gently.

3 Season with salt to taste, and enjoy!

DAY

4

Today is your day. You should feel fully energized and totally comfortable with this new way of eating. My hope is that, as you return gradually to your former eating habits, you will take with you several of your new habits, the most important of which is drinking a green juice every morning.

1 glass of lemon water (12 ounces/355ml)

Your bowels should be running like clock-work now, allowing you to fully absorb the nutrients from all the wonderful fruits and vegetables you're consuming. Keep up your water habit first thing in the morning—not just during a cleanse, but for every single day of your life.

1 cup of green tea (8 ounces/235ml)

Still optional. If you don't need the caffeine, skip it.

1 glass of Fall Morning Green Juice (16 ounces/475ml) (see recipe on page 123)

Did you wake up craving your morning greens? You should notice a definite change in your "green palate" since the first day of your cleanse. If your morning green juice tastes too sweet, that means you have suc-ceeded in cleansing your body of the toxins that lead to sweet cravings. Good for you! If you continue to drink a green juice every morning, you can use less and less fruit and move toward a purely green juice (no fruit included). Try cutting the apple in half today.

red bell pepper
JUICE

Full of vitamin C and other antioxidants, red peppers enhance both the healthfulness and taste of an already nutritious green juice.

Optional lunch addition: 1 cup (150g) of chopped red peppers. *Eat the chopped peppers if your lunch juice doesn't satiate you.*

INGREDIENTS

3 to 5 celery stalks, bottoms removed

Big handful of spinach (⅔ bunch)

2 to 3 romaine (cos) leaves

1 red bell pepper (red capsicum)

Handful of parsley leaves (from 3 to 4 stems)

¼ lemon, peeled (optional)

1 Wash the celery, spinach, romaine, bell pepper, and parsley.

2 Remove the top and seeds from the bell pepper and cut into pieces that will fit through your juicer.

3 If you need to cut the greenness, use ¼ lemon. If not, skip it.

4 Run all ingredients through your juicer, scrape off foam (if desired), and enjoy!

broccoli green
JUICE

When my son, Cooper, was young, I used to steam broccoli for him, and he would eat only the tops—or the "trees," as he called them. One day, I threw a leftover stalk in the juicer with my morning green juice. I was hooked.

Optional snack addition: 1 cup (85g) of broccoli florets and cucumber slices (sprinkled with sea salt to taste). *Only snack on these extra veggies if you're not satiated after your mid-afternoon juice.*

INGREDIENTS

1 cucumber

3 celery stalks, bottoms removed

3 to 4 kale leaves

½ stalk of broccoli (no floret)

Handful of basil (6 to 7 leaves)

½ lemon, peeled (optional)

1 Wash the cucumber, celery, kale, broccoli, and basil.

2 If you need to cut the greenness, use ½ lemon. If not, skip it.

3 Run all ingredients through your juicer, scrape off foam (if desired), and enjoy!

SUPERFOOD HIGHLIGHT:
broccoli

With an impressive lineup of nutrients, including high quantities of vitamins A and C, broccoli is also packed with potassium, calcium, and iron. Researchers are constantly studying the wonderful cancer-fighting potential of broccoli along with its ability to help lower cholesterol. Broccoli also contains the all-important vitamin D, a vitamin in which many Americans are deficient. To store, place broccoli in a plastic bag, removing as much of the air from the bag as possible. It should stay fresh in the fridge for up to ten days, but be sure to store it dry.

Time for some delicious raw soup! This recipe is a raw version of my favorite holiday vegetable dish, which I prepare for both Thanksgiving and Christmas. The cooked version involves baked butternut squash garnished with dried or fresh cranberries and wilted garlic spinach. I was determined to re-create these wonderful flavors in the form of a raw soup. If you've been using a Vitamix, you should now be deeply in love. It's a fantastic tool for making soups. If you don't have one, use a high-speed blender. By this point in the cleanse, you may want a little something warm in your tummy, so I recommend the extra step of heating this soup a bit on the stove.

INGREDIENTS

½ small butternut squash, peeled and cubed

½ medium avocado or 1 small avocado

1 cup (235ml) filtered water

1 tbsp extra-virgin olive oil

2 tbsp maple syrup

1 garlic clove

Sea salt and pepper, to taste

Handful of dried cranberries (for garnish)

raw butternut squash SOUP

1 Combine the butternut squash, avocado meat, water, olive oil, maple syrup, and garlic in a high-speed blender or Vitamix.

2 Blend on High until smooth, adding more water as needed until it reaches desired consistency.

3 Season with salt and pepper to taste.

4 If you would like a warm soup while keeping it raw, pour it into a saucepan on the stove and heat over the lowest possible temperature. Stir constantly until the soup is warm to the touch, and remove immediately. Ladle into a bowl and garnish with pepper and dried cranberries.

Living in Texas, I have rosemary that grows like a weed year-round in my front yard. Since this is the only herb that I seem to be able to grow in this climate, I decided to incorporate it into a salad. While it is certainly an unusual ingredient for a salad, I think it adds a fun taste and texture. Just make sure to chop it very finely, and don't use too much.

crunchy rosemary
SALAD

INGREDIENTS

Bowl of baby mixed greens (such as red and green romaine [cos])

Handful of tarragon leaves (from 2 to 3 stems), finely chopped

Handful of rosemary leaves (from 1 to 2 stems), finely chopped

Juice of ½ lime

2 tbsp hempseed

2 tbsp almond oil

Sea salt, to taste

4 to 5 raw crackers, broken into bits

1 avocado, thinly sliced

1 Combine the mixed greens, tarragon, and rosemary in a salad bowl and toss.

2 Add the lime juice, hempseed, and almond oil, and toss again.

3 Season with salt to taste. Add crackers and toss gently.

4 Arrange a layer of avocado slices over the top, and enjoy!

🕐 TIME SAVER

While I love eating raw, I draw the line at dehydrating my own crackers. Luckily, a number of great brands have started making wonderful raw crackers—including Two Moms in the Raw.

CONGRATS! You have successfully completed your Fall 4-Day Green Juice and Raw Food Cleanse. Your intestines, body, and mind should be thanking you now. You should be feeling more energized than ever. In addition, you should notice that you have enhanced mental clarity and even a nice glow to your skin. For information and recipes that will help you maintain the wonderful benefits of your cleanse and help you transition to post-cleanse eating, please turn to page 149.

maintaining
POST-CLEANSE

Congrats on completing your 4-Day Cleanse! If this is your first cleanse, then extra congratulations are in order. You may be asking yourself: Now what?! This chapter will provide a detailed roadmap for easing back into more mainstream eating, while at the same time maintaining some of your newfound healthy eating habits.

You should now be a champion juicer. Hopefully you have perfected your Morning Green Juice. If you only pick up one habit during your cleanse, make it this one. Drinking a green juice every morning should be a lifelong routine—and it'll pay off for the rest of your life. If you are burned out on using your juicer, switch to a bottle of ready-made Daily Greens juice. Any of the Daily Greens green juices are a great substitute for a homemade juice. They also have a longer shelf life, as a result of the high-pressure process (HPP) used to make them FDA compliant and grocery-store ready. This process does not reduce any nutrients, but it does kill the bacteria that normally start the fermentation process, thereby extending the shelf life significantly. You should also continue your morning routine of drinking a 12-ounce (355 ml) glass of water with lemon upon rising. And if you're up for it, I strongly recommend you stay off the coffee and continue having a cup of green tea in the morning.

DAY 1

On your first day post cleanse, whatever you do, please do not go out and eat a hamburger or other hefty serving of meat. You will seriously regret it. It It is best to transition slowly back to eating animal protein, dairy, and grains. The benefits achieved over the past four days can be compromised if you suddenly jump right back into your old dietary habits. This can have a negative effect on the energy and feeling of well-being created during the juice cleanse.

For lunch on your first day post-cleanse, I highly recommend sticking with a raw salad. A good choice would be one of your favorite dinner salads from the cleanse. However, any raw salad will work. If you are eating out at a restaurant, which is always fun after eating at home for four days, just order the biggest salad on the menu and ask them to hold the grains, cheese, and animal protein. You will not be ready for these yet. Stay light and skip the animal protein today.

For dinner, I recommend moving gradually back into cooked food by consuming a plant-based cooked dinner. This will ease you back into your more typical diet without burdening your digestive system with heavier meals consisting of grains and animal proteins. Some recipes appropriate for your first post-cleanse dinner can be found in this chapter.

It is worth noting that this Day 1 post-cleanse menu is actually the way I usually eat on a day-to-day basis. While I maintain a 100 percent plant-based diet, I do not eat 100 percent raw. There is great benefit, I find, in cooking some vegetables that are not palatable in their raw form. For example, potatoes, legumes, and whole grains would all be missing from my diet because they're inedible raw, yet these foods supply vital nutrients, including protein, to a plant-based diet. However, I do try to limit my consumption of "cooked" plants: I only eat them in my evening meal. This type of diet is commonly referred to as "raw until dinner." If you're still fired up from your 4-Day Cleanse and want to continue with this way of eating, linger as long as you want in the raw-until-dinner phase. I love it so much that I have adopted it as my lifelong way of eating.

DAY 2

On Day 2 post-cleanse, I usually recommend slowly reintroducing grains and dairy—that is, if you plan to go back to consuming dairy at all. Dairy has the potential to be inflammatory if you have sensitivities to it. This inflammation can cause some individuals to experience bloating, indigestion, and allergy symptoms.

As stated previously, in the morning I hope you will continue your routine of a glass of lemon water, followed by green tea (instead of coffee) and a glass of Morning Green Juice. Midday, even when you fully return to a more normalized diet, I recommend that you consider eating much lighter for lunch. Consider how great you have felt on your cleanse during the day. Save the animal protein and grains for dinner. For three additional raw vegetable salads that are hearty and should assist you in assimilating, see pages 153–155.

For dinner on your second day post-cleanse, I recommend adding back cooked grains or easy-to-digest animal protein like eggs. However, I would pick either grains or eggs to add to dinner, not both.

DAY 3

If a salad is not cutting it for you for lunch, try adding grains to lunch by swapping out your salad for a whole-grain vegetable sandwich. I make a mean Hungry Girl Sandwich (or Hungry Guy Sandwich,

as the case may be; see page 156) that would fill up and satiate a linebacker. By incorporating cooked whole grains back into your lunch, you will feel more satiated. For a couple of hearty vegetable sandwiches that will make you very happy, see pages 156–157.

On Day 3, I recommend reintroducing fish or meat. While I am 100 percent plant-based, it is not something that I necessarily recommend for others. For most, it is difficult to feel fulfilled and satiated by a diet consisting solely of plants. However, I would encourage you to consider eating less meat in your day-to-day diet. Try limiting your fish or meat consumption to only dinner.

And if you are going to consume animal protein, I recommend fish over any other kind. It is lower in bad fats, while still containing lots of the good stuff like healthy omega-3 and omega-6 fatty acids. But don't forget your veggies! Consider eating a cooked vegetable meal with meat or fish as your side dish, focusing on your newfound love for vegetables.

I love the combination of oranges and pomegranate seeds in the winter with sweet winter kale. This salad is so fun to make with winter/early spring kale from the farmers market.

INGREDIENTS

1 orange

2 tbsp extra-virgin olive oil

1-inch (2.5 cm) piece ginger root, minced

1 tsp agave nectar

4 to 5 kale leaves, torn into bite-size pieces

Sea salt and pepper, to taste

½ lemon

1 pomegranate, seeds only

¼ cup (30g) almond slivers

kale orange
SALAD

1 Peel the orange and remove slices from the membrane, collecting the juice as you do so. Set aside the orange slices.

2 To make the dressing, whisk together the orange juice, olive oil, ginger, and agave nectar in a small bowl. Set aside.

3 Place the kale leaves in a salad bowl and season with salt and pepper.

4 Squeeze lemon juice onto the kale leaves, and massage the juice into the kale to break it down a bit.

5 Toss in orange slices, pomegranate seeds, and almond slivers.

6 Pour the dressing over the salad and toss gently. Season with more salt and pepper to taste, and enjoy!

Sometimes, a good old-fashioned sandwich really hits the spot. When making a sandwich, I always try to use whole-grain breads instead of refined breads. One favorite is the sprouted Ezekiel grain breads made by Food for Life. Because the grains are sprouted, they have more nutrients than regular grains plus additional fiber. I find them very filling.

INGREDIENTS

2 slices of sprouted-grain bread

1 tbsp Veganaise dressing (such as Follow Your Heart brand)

½ avocado, sliced

½ medium tomato, sliced

1 to 2 butter lettuce leaves

1 to 2 basil leaves

Handful of sprouts (any kind)

shauna's hungry girl (OR GUY) SANDWICH

1 Spread the sprouted-grain slices with Veganaise.

2 Add the avocado and tomato slices.

3 Layer on the lettuce and basil leaves.

4 Add sprouts, close up the sandwich, and enjoy.

portobello mushroom
SANDWICH

D/G

I love grilled portobello mush-rooms, and they make a very hearty sandwich with tons of flavor. This recipe has a few more steps than my usual recipe, but trust me, it's worth it!

INGREDIENTS

1 portobello mushroom

1 tbsp balsamic vinegar

4 tbsp extra-virgin olive oil, divided

½ red bell pepper (red capsicum), sliced

Sea salt and black pepper, to taste

1 big bunch of basil

¼ cup (35g) pine nuts

2 slices of whole-grain bread (preferably sprouted grain)

1 Preheat the oven to 400°F (200°C).

2 To marinate the mushroom, pour balsamic vinegar and 1 tablespoon of olive oil into the center of the upside-down mushroom and let stand for a few minutes.

3 Brush the bell pepper slices with olive oil and season with salt and pepper.

4 Place the mushroom and red pepper into a baking dish, cover with foil, and bake for about 20 minutes or until both are tender.

5 To make a vegan pesto, combine the basil, pine nuts, and remaining 2 to 3 tablespoons of olive oil in a high-speed blender or Vitamix. Blend on high until smooth, approximately one minute. Season with salt and pepper to taste. Add more oil as needed to reach desired consistency.

6 When ready to prepare your sandwich, toast the bread and coat each slice with pesto.

7 Layer the mushroom and roasted red peppers onto one slice of bread, close up your sandwich, and enjoy!

When you are vegan, you learn that it is best to bring your own dish to all potluck events, especially brunch events in Texas, which tend to mostly consist of bacon and egg tacos. My good friend Jennifer Anderson introduced me to this wonderful plant-based casserole, which is always a huge hit at potlucks, particularly at brunch, but also makes for a very filling dinner dish. Allow yourself about forty-five minutes baking time, but it takes less than ten minutes to prep.

INGREDIENTS

2 sweet potatoes, peeled and cubed

1 bunch of green asparagus, cut into 3-inch pieces

3 to 4 garlic cloves, minced

Handful of fresh thyme leaves (from 2 to 3 sprigs), finely chopped

1 to 2 plant-based sausages (such as Field Roast brand)

3 to 4 tbsp extra-virgin olive oil

Sea salt and pepper, to taste

winter sweet potato-asparagus
CASSEROLE

1 Preheat the oven to 425°F (220°C).

2 Arrange the sweet potatoes in a glass casserole dish.

3 Arrange the asparagus on top, then sprinkle with garlic and thyme.

4 Break up the sausage into bite-size chunks and sprinkle over the top.

5 Drizzle olive oil over the casserole, distributing evenly across the surface. Season with salt and pepper.

6 Place foil over the casserole and bake for 45 minutes or until the sweet potatoes are soft. Remove foil and bake a few more minutes until everything is a bit crispy.

I came up with this recipe one day on the fly, when I didn't have time to hit the grocery store and only had a random assortment of vegetables in my crisper drawer. It turned out so great that this is one of my frequent standbys when I'm in a hurry and the fridge isn't fully stocked. I simply use what I have on hand and mix and match the veggies for an Asian-inspired stir-fry. This recipe uses my favorite veggies, but almost any vegetable can serve as an acceptable substitute.

asian
STIR-FRY

INGREDIENTS

½ container firm tofu

3 tbsp sesame oil, divided

3 tbsp raw almond butter, divided

4 to 5 tbsp raw soy sauce (nama shoyu), divided

2 garlic cloves, minced

1 tbsp minced fresh ginger root

2 to 3 green (spring) onions, thinly sliced

1 head bok choy (or cabbage or zucchini), roughly chopped

3 mushrooms (any kind), roughly chopped

1 cup (70g) broccoli florets, chopped

½ medium carrot, thinly sliced or shredded

Dash of cayenne to taste (optional)

Handful of cilantro (coriander) leaves (from 5 to 6 stems), torn into pieces

1 Squeeze the excess water out of the tofu and cut into bite-sized chunks.

2 Heat 1 tablespoon of sesame oil in a wok or large nonstick sauté pan over high heat.

3 Add 1 tablespoon of almond butter, 1 tablespoon of soy sauce, and tofu to wok and stir until tofu is crispy on the outside. Remove from wok and set aside.

4 Add remaining sesame oil, remaining almond butter, garlic, ginger, and green onions. Stir until crispy.

5 Add all the remaining vegetables and stir constantly.

6 After a couple minutes, add the remaining soy sauce. If desired, sprinkle with a dash of cayenne to add spice.

7 Stir until vegetables are crispy but not fully cooked. (You don't want to cook all the nutrients out of your vegetables.) When vegetables are almost done, toss in the tofu and stir until warm.

8 Remove from heat and serve garnished with cilantro.

summer grilled
SALAD

During the summer, all my friends and family are usually grilling burgers and hot dogs outdoors. Not wanting to miss out on the fun, I decided to come up with my own grilled plant-based dish.

INGREDIENTS

1 head of romaine (cos) lettuce

1 head of radicchio lettuce

4 to 5 tbsp extra-virgin olive oil

Sea salt and black cracked pepper, to taste

1 package (roll) of polenta

1 tbsp raw apple cider vinegar (I recommend Bragg's)

1 tbsp whole-grain mustard

1 green (spring) onion, thinly sliced

1 Prep the grill to normal grilling temperature.

2 Separate the romaine leaves and chop the head of radicchio in half. Brush each leaf and each radicchio half with olive oil and sprinkle with salt and pepper.

3 Slice the roll of polenta lengthwise into three or four slices that are each about 1-inch (2.5 cm) thick. Brush the polenta slices with olive oil and sprinkle with salt and pepper.

4 To prepare a dip or dressing for the grilled vegetables, combine 3 tablespoons of olive oil with the apple cider vinegar, mustard, and green onion, and whisk until well mixed.

5 Grill the lettuce and polenta, taking care not to burn them. The lettuce should just be wilted in order to get a grilled flavor.

6 Roughly chop the grilled romaine, radicchio, and polenta, and combine on a plate or serving platter.

7 Pour the dressing over the salad and toss, or use as a dip.

autumn butternut squash
WITH SPINACH

D/G

...so I wanted to bring something special. This dish has become such a hit that now I often make it for holiday gatherings. I have sized this recipe down to make a hearty dinner for one.

INGREDIENTS

½ butternut squash, seeded

3 tbsp extra-virgin olive oil, divided

1 tbsp maple syrup

2 tbsp dried cranberries

2 tbsp pine nuts

1 bunch of spinach, stems removed, or 1 bag of baby spinach

2 to 3 garlic cloves, minced

1 Preheat the oven to 425°F (220°C).

2 Place the squash half into a small glass casserole dish and add 1 tablespoon of olive oil and maple syrup into the center hole of the squash.

3 Cover with foil and bake for 45 minutes or until squash is soft (check for doneness by inserting a knife into thickest portion of squash to make sure it is soft all the way through).

4 Meanwhile, in a medium nonstick sauté pan, sauté the cranberries and pine nuts in 1 tablespoon of olive oil until the pine nuts are brown. Remove and set aside.

5 Heat the remaining olive oil in the same sauté pan. Add the minced garlic and sauté for 1 minute or until brown.

6 Add the spinach and sauté for 2 to 3 minutes, mixing with the garlic, until the spinach is wilted but not cooked.

7 To serve, place the butternut squash on a plate or serving platter and arrange the wilted spinach around the outside. Sprinkle the squash with pine nuts and cranberries, and enjoy!

Although I don't eat eggs myself anymore, I do prepare them frequently for my husband and son. Eggs are a wonderful source of protein. Out of all the animal proteins, they are the most easily digested and assimilated by the body. As such, eggs are a great transition food as you move back into heavier animal proteins. (Plus, it's fun to eat eggs for dinner instead of breakfast!) Skip the toast, and eat these delicious eggs with vegetables instead.

warm spinach & eggs

(aka breakfast for dinner)

INGREDIENTS

2 to 3 eggs

Dash of cayenne pepper (optional)

2 tbsp olive oil, divided

1 green (spring) onion, thinly sliced

1 to 2 garlic cloves, minced

1 bunch of spinach, stems removed, or 1 bag of baby spinach

1 Whisk the eggs, and add a dash of cayenne if you like spice.

2 Heat 1 tablespoon of olive oil in a sauté pan over medium heat. Scramble the eggs, being sure not to overcook them. Set aside on a plate.

3 In the same pan, add the remaining olive oil, green onions, and garlic and cook for 1 minute or until slightly brown.

4 Add the spinach and cook for a minute or two, until wilted but not fully cooked.

5 Arrange the spinach on the plate of scrambled eggs, and enjoy!

Soba noodles are my go-to noodle because they are made from buckwheat and are therefore gluten-free. I love to combine them with any vegetables, but I am especially inspired to do so with fresh spring vegetables and herbs for a fun Asian-inspired noodle bowl.

INGREDIENTS

1 package of soba noodles

Sea salt, for boiling water

1 cucumber, peeled and thinly sliced or shredded

1 small carrot, thinly sliced or shredded

1 green (spring) onion, thinly sliced

½-inch (1.25 cm) piece ginger root, minced

2 tbsp sesame oil

1 tbsp rice wine vinegar

1 tbsp maple syrup

2 tbsp raw soy sauce (nama shoyu)

1 tbsp black sesame seeds

Sprinkle of red pepper flakes (dried chili flakes), to taste (optional)

Handful of mung bean sprouts

Handful of basil (6 to 7 leaves), chopped

Handful of cilantro (coriander) leaves (from 5 to 6 stems), chopped

Handful of mint (6 to 7 leaves), chopped

asian spring soba
NOODLES

1 Boil the soba noodles according to the package directions, adding a bit of salt to really bring out the flavors. Drain and place in a large bowl.

2 Add the cucumber, carrot, and green onion to the soba noodles and toss to combine.

3 To make an Asian vinaigrette, whisk together the ginger root, sesame oil, rice wine vinegar, maple syrup, soy sauce, sesame seeds, and red pepper flakes in a separate bowl.

4 Pour the dressing over the noodles and vegetables and toss until everything is coated.

5 Add the mung bean sprouts and herbs to the noodle bowl and serve warm or chilled.

summer quinoa
SALAD

Quinoa is a wonderful grain that is high in protein. As a result, it is a wonderful addition to a plant-based diet and is far superior to other grains, which do not contain very much protein. This salad makes a fantastic summer treat using colorful summer vegetables from the farmers market.

INGREDIENTS

1 cup (170g) quinoa

1 medium carrot, shredded or diced, or ½ cup (60g) shredded carrots

½ red pepper (red capsicum), finely diced

½ yellow pepper (yellow capsicum), finely diced

½ cup (35g) green cabbage, shredded

½ cup (35g) red cabbage, shredded

Handful of cilantro (coriander) leaves (from 5 to 6 stems), torn into pieces

Handful of basil (6 to 7 leaves), torn into pieces

2 tbsp sesame oil

1 tbsp raw coconut vinegar or rice vinegar

½-inch (1.25 cm) piece ginger root, minced

1 tbsp black sesame seeds

1 Rinse and boil the quinoa for about 15 minutes, or until soft (or follow instructions on package). Transfer to a salad bowl.

2 Combine all vegetables and herbs with the quinoa and toss well.

3 To make the dressing, whisk together the sesame oil, vinegar, ginger, and sesame seeds.

4 Pour the dressing over the quinoa-vegetable mix and toss gently until everything is coated.

Wheatberries are the hard kernels from the wheat plant. They are the whole grain, containing the bran, germ, and endosperm. Because they are not refined in any way and are a great source of fiber, I love combining them with fall vegetables for a filling fall meal. Wheatberries need to soak overnight, so keep that in mind if you're going to make this delicious treat.

INGREDIENTS

1 cup (180g) raw wheatberries, soaked overnight

1 acorn squash (or butternut squash), peeled and cubed

3 tbsp extra-virgin olive oil, divided

Sea salt and pepper, to taste

1 tbsp raw whole-grain mustard

1 tbsp maple syrup

1 tsp lemon juice

¼ cup (40g) dried cranberries

½ bag of baby spinach or arugula (rocket) (or combination of both)

autumn acorn squash & wheatberry
SALAD

1 Boil the wheatberries until soft and edible. This can take up to 30 minutes.

2 Preheat the oven to 425°F (220°C).

3 Combine the acorn squash with 1 tablespoon olive oil and salt and pepper to taste.

4 Transfer to a baking dish or baking sheet and cover with foil. Bake for 30 minutes or until squash is soft. To check for doneness, insert a knife into a squash cube.

5 To make the dressing, whisk together the remaining 2 tablespoons of olive oil, mustard, maple syrup, and lemon juice in a small bowl.

6 When the wheatberries are done, drain and transfer to a salad bowl.

7 Pour the dressing over the wheatberries and toss to coat.

8 Add the squash and cranberries and toss gently.

9 Add the spinach or arugula and toss gently to combine. Serve hot or cold.

ACKNOWLEDGMENTS

Thank you to Mayim Bialik for being such a wonderful supporter and to Lauren Minchen for all that you do for Daily Greens.

Thank you to the entire Daily Greens team. You all inspire me each and every day!

Finally, thank you to my ever-supportive husband, Kirk, and my beautiful son, Cooper. You are my sunshine, my reason for being, my everything!

ABOUT THE AUTHOR

Shauna R. Martin is CEO and founder of Daily Greens, a raw, cold-pressed green juice company based in Austin, Texas. In 2005, Shauna was diagnosed with breast cancer. With a young family to care for, she turned to daily green juicing to recover from the trauma of multiple surgeries and the toxic effects of chemotherapy. After discovering the life-restoring power of green juices, she made it her mission to get them into the hands of everyone that she could, so that all could thrive as she has.

In 2012, after an eighteen-year career as a corporate attorney, Shauna founded Drink Daily Greens LLC. Dedicated to sharing the benefits of green juices with as many people as possible, Shauna devotes her time to crafting new, delicious recipes and selling her Daily Greens beverages, which are available in retail outlets nationwide.

An active advocate for breast cancer issues, Shauna has served on the Board of the Breast Cancer Resource Centers of Texas for the past eight years (she was President of the Board for two years and is currently Chair of the Development Committee). She is also a founding member of the Pink Ribbon Cowgirls, a social network of young breast cancer survivors, as well as a frequent speaker and chair of breast cancer fundraising awards. In furtherance of Shauna's mission, 1 percent of sales of Daily Greens is granted to fund organizations that provide services to young women and underserved women battling breast cancer.

Shauna lives in Austin, drinking her veggies, with her husband, Kirk, and their ten-year-old son, Cooper.

ABOUT THE CONTRIBUTORS

Mayim Hoya Bialik is best known for her lead role as Blossom Russo in the early-1990s NBC television sitcom *Blossom*. She currently plays the role of Amy Farrah Fowler on the hit CBS comedy *The Big Bang Theory*, a role for which she has received 3 consecutive Emmy nominations. After *Blossom*, Bialik took a break from acting to earn a BS and PhD in Neuroscience from UCLA. She is the author of *Beyond the Sling* (2012) and *Mayim's Vegan Table* (2014).

Lauren Minchen is a Registered Dietitian/Nutritionist in New York City. She has a wide range of professional experience in nutrition-related diseases and conditions, including eating disorders, digestive diseases, hormonal disorders, cancer, autoimmune diseases, sports nutrition, and pre-and post-natal nutrition. At Lauren Minchen Nutrition, Lauren takes a holistic approach, providing clients with one-on-one consulting and counseling sessions. She also offers her expertise as a consultant on nutritional supplements and other nutrition-related topics.

INDEX

algae
  blue-green algae juice, 57
  freshwater blue-green algae, 56
almond butter wraps, 42
antioxidants, 7, 8, 22, 38, 46, 50, 56,
  66, 75, 94, 102, 122, 132, 143
arugula
  autumn acorn squash & wheatberry
    salad, 171
  cherry tomato & avocado salad, 99
  super greens & mint salad, 77
  watercress arugula salad, 83
Asian spring soba noodles, 166, 167
Asian stir-fry, 160, 161
autumn acorn squash & wheatberry
  salad, 170, 171
autumn butternut squash with spinach, 163
avocado
  avocado cup, 139, 140
  avocado tomato delight, 53
  cherry tomato & avocado salad, 99
  collard green wraps, 76
  creamy avocado smoothie, 28
  crunchy rosemary salad, 147
  fall fennel salad, 129
  glowing skin smoothie, 29
  heavenly herb salad, 141
  raw bok choy salad, 89
  raw butternut squash soup, 145
  raw carrot soup, 127
  raw guacamole & veggies, 98
  raw guacamole tacos, 135
  raw kale salad, 115
  romaine lettuce wraps, 117
  Shauna's hungry girl (or guy)
    sandwich, 156
  summer coleslaw, 104
  sweet nori wrap, 47
  veggie hand rolls, 48
  winter grapefruit salad, 43

blood orange & pomegranate endive
  cups, 70, 71
bok choy
  bok choy green juice, 86
  raw bok choy salad, 88, 89
broccoli
  broccoli green juice, 144
  nutrition information, 144

cabbage
  Asian stir-fry, 160

cabbage green juice, 56
raw kimchi, 87
red cabbage & walnut salad, 72
summer coleslaw, 104
summer quinoa salad, 169
Caesar salad, vegan, 110, 111
cantaloupe-zucchini green juice, 106
carrot
  carrot-cilantro green juice, 80, 81
  carrot-pineapple green juice, 74
  chard-carrot green juice, 50
  orange-carrot juice with greens,
    131
  raw carrot soup, 126, 127
cauliflower soup, raw, 58, 59
cherry tomato & avocado salad, 99
chia seeds
  kale-grape-melon smoothie, 31
  melon green juice with, 96
  nutrition information, 96
  summer greens smoothie, 30
cilantro, 26, 36, 37, 39, 41, 43, 45, 79,
  81, 92, 93, 98, 102, 107, 121, 133,
  135, 141, 160, 166, 169
coleslaw, summer, 104
collard greens, 16, 21,
  collard green wraps, 76
  summer morning green juice, 95
  super green juice, 85
  sweet collard greens summer salad,
    155
coriander (cilantro), 26, 36, 37, 39, 41,
  43, 45, 79, 81, 92, 93, 98, 102, 107,
  121, 133, 135, 141, 160, 166, 169
cos, 33, 36, 37, 39, 40, 41, 42, 48, 64,
  65, 75, 76, 85, 93, 111, 117, 120,
  121, 124, 129, 132, 135, 141, 143,
  147, 162
creamy avocado smoothie, 28
cucumber
  heirloom tomatoes & cucumber
    salad, 154
  watermelon cucumber salad, 103

dandelion greens
  dandelion green juice, 114
  nutrition information, 114
"Dirty Dozen Plus," 19

eggs, warm spinach &, 165
equipment needed, 20–22
exercise, 10, 12, 23

fall 4-day green juice & raw food
  cleanse, 119–148

day 1, 122–129
day 2, 130–135
day 3, 136–141
day 4, 142–148
shopping lists, 120, 121
fall fennel salad, 128, 129
fennel-apple green juice, 125
foods to eliminate, 20
formula, simple green juice, 21
frequently asked questions, 23

gazpacho, 108, 109
ginger, sweet greens juice with, 69
glowing skin smoothie, 29
grape
  kale-grape green juice, 132
  kale-grape-melon smoothie, 31
grapefruit
  vanilla-grapefruit green juice, 45
  winter grapefruit salad, 43
green juice, 16–17
  broccoli green juice, 144
  cabbage green juice, 56
  carrot-cilantro green juice, 80, 81
  chard-carrot green juice, 50
  dandelion green juice, 114
  fall morning green juice, 123, 130,
    136, 142
  fennel-apple green juice, 125
  formula, 21
  honeydew-watercress green juice,
    107
  kale-grape green juice, 132
  kale-zucchini green juice, 137
  kiwi green juice, 40
  melon green juice with chia seeds,
    96
  New Year morning green juice, 39,
    44, 49, 55
  peach green juice, 101
  pear-vanilla green juice, 79
  pineapple-carrot green juice, 74
  pineapple-jalapeño green juice,
    138
  pineapple-mint green juice, 68
  pineapple with greens juice, 124
  Shauna's daily morning greens
    juice, 32, 33
  spicy winter green juice, 52
  spring morning green juice, 67, 73,
    78, 84
  strawberry green juice, 75
  summer morning green juice, 95,
    100, 105, 112
  super green juice, 85

sweet greens juice with ginger, 69
sweet honeydew green juice, 97
vanilla-grapefruit green juice, 45
watercress green juice, 46
zucchini-cantaloupe green juice, 106
zucchini-pear green juice with cilantro, 102
green smoothie, 22
creamy avocado smoothie, 28
glowing skin smoothie, 29
kale-grape-melon smoothie, 31
Shauna's green smoothie, 24, 25
simple green smoothie, 27
spicy pineapple-kale smoothie, 26
summer greens smoothie, 30
green tea, 7, 12, 22
guacamole, 98, 135

hand rolls, veggie, 48
heavenly herb salad, 141
heirloom tomatoes & cucumber salad, 154
honeydew
honeydew-watercress green juice, 107
sweet honeydew green juice, 97
hydration, 7–8, 18, 20, 38, 49, 66, 78, 94, 96, 105, 122, 136, 147

jalapeño-pineapple green juice, 138
juices, *see under individual ingredient or recipe name*

kale, 12, 16, 21, 132
blue-green algae juice, 57
broccoli green juice, 144
carrot-cilantro green juice, 81
carrot-pineapple green juice, 74
cherry tomato & avocado salad, 99
fall morning green juice, 123
fennel-apple green juice, 125
kale-grape green juice, 132
kale-grape-melon smoothie, 31
kale orange salad, 153
kale-zucchini green juice, 137
New Year morning green juice, 39
nutrition information, 132
orange-romaine green juice, 41
pineapple-jalapeño green juice, 138
raw kale salad, 115
Shauna's daily morning greens juice, 33
spicy pineapple-kale smoothie, 26

summer morning green juice, 95
super greens & mint salad, 77
sweet collard greens summer salad, 155
sweet greens juice with ginger, 69
types of, 132
vanilla-grapefruit green juice, 45
winter grapefruit salad, 43
yellow bell pepper juice, 113
kiwi green juice, 40

melon
honeydew-watercress green juice, 107
kale-grape-melon smoothie, 31
melon green juice with chia seeds, 96
simple green juice formula, 21
summer morning green juice, 95
sweet honeydew green juice, 97
watermelon cucumber salad, 103
zucchini-cantaloupe green juice, 106
mint, 21, 64, 65, 92, 93, 105, 121
Asian spring soba noodles, 166
heavenly herb salad, 141
melon green juice with chia seeds, 96
peach green juice, 101
pineapple-mint green juice, 68
Shauna's green smoothie, 25
strawberry green juice, 75
summer morning green juice, 95
super greens & mint salad, 77
watermelon cucumber salad, 103
mixed radish slices, 82
morning green juice, *see green juice and individual recipe name*

New Year 4-day green juice & raw food cleanse, 35–62
day 1, 38–43
day 2, 44–48
day 3, 49–54
day 4, 55–62
shopping lists, 36, 37
noodles, Asian spring soba, 166, 167

orange
blood orange & pomegranate endive cups, 70, 71
kale orange salad, 153
orange-carrot juice with greens, 131
orange-romaine green juice, 41

peach green juice, 101
pear
pear-vanilla green juice, 79
zucchini-pear green juice with cilantro, 102
pineapple
carrot-pineapple green juice, 74
pineapple-jalapeño green juice, 138
pineapple-mint green juice, 68
pineapple with greens juice, 124
spicy pineapple-kale smoothie, 26
portobello mushroom sandwich, 157

quinoa salad, summer, 168, 169

raw bok choy salad, 88, 89
raw butternut squash soup, 145
raw carrot soup, 126, 127
raw cauliflower soup, 58, 59
raw fruits and vegetables, 7, 8, 18, 22
raw guacamole & veggies, 98
raw guacamole tacos, 135
raw kale salad, 115
raw kimchi, 87
raw salsa & veggies, 133
raw zucchini spaghetti, 54
red bell pepper juice, 143
red cabbage & walnut salad, 72
red capsicum, 65, 76, 93, 98, 120, 121, 127, 133, 143, 157, 169
rocket, 65, 77, 83, 99, 171
romaine lettuce, 21
almond butter wraps, 42
collard green wraps, 76
crunchy rosemary salad, 147
fall fennel salad, 129
heavenly herb salad, 141
kale-grape green juice, 132
kiwi green juice, 40
New Year morning green juice, 39
orange-romaine green juice, 41
pineapple with greens juice, 124
raw guacamole tacos, 135
red bell pepper juice, 143
romaine lettuce wraps, 116, 117
Shauna's daily morning greens juice, 33
strawberry green juice, 75
summer grilled salad, 162
super green juice, 85
vegan Caesar salad, 111
veggie hand rolls, 48
rosemary salad, crunchy 146, 147

salad
    autumn acorn squash & wheatberry
      salad, 170, 171
    cherry tomato & avocado salad, 99
    crunchy rosemary salad, 146, 147
    fall fennel salad, 128, 129
    heavenly herb salad, 141
    heirloom tomatoes & cucumber
      salad, 154
    kale orange salad, 153
    raw bok choy salad, 88, 89
    raw kale salad, 115
    red cabbage & walnut salad, 72
    simple winter salad, 60, 61
    summer grilled salad, 162
    summer quinoa salad, 168, 169
    super greens & mint salad, 77
    sweet collard greens summer salad,
      155
    vegan Caesar salad, 110, 111
    watercress arugula salad, 83
    watermelon cucumber salad, 103
    winter grapefruit salad, 43
salsa & veggies, raw, 133
sandwich
    portobello mushroom sandwich,
      157
    Shauna's hungry girl (or guy) sand-
      wich, 150–151, 156
simple green juice formula, 21
simple green smoothie, 27
simple winter salad, 60, 61
smoothies, *see* green smoothies
soup
    gazpacho, 108, 109
    raw butternut squash soup, 145
    raw carrot soup, 126, 127
    raw cauliflower soup, 58, 59
spaghetti, raw zucchini, 54
spicy pineapple-kale smoothie, 26
spicy winter green juice, 52
spinach, 16, 19
    autumn acorn squash & wheatberry
      salad, 171
    autumn butternut squash with
      spinach, 163
    bok choy green juice, 86
    chard-carrot green juice, 50
    cherry tomato and avocado salad,
      99
    creamy avocado smoothie, 28
    dandelion green juice, 114
    glowing skin smoothie, 29
    melon green juice with chia
      seeds, 96

nutrition information, 106
orange-carrot juice with greens,
    131
peach green juice, 101
pear-vanilla green juice, 79
pineapple-mint green juice, 68
raw butternut squash soup, 145
red bell pepper juice, 143
Shauna's green smoothie, 25
simple green juice formula, 21
simple green smoothie, 27
spicy winter green juice, 52
spring morning green juice, 67
strawberry green juice, 75
summer greens smoothie, 30
super greens & mint salad, 77
sweet honeydew green juice, 97
warm spinach & eggs, 165
watercress green juice, 46
zucchini-cantaloupe green juice,
    106
zucchini-pear green juice with
    cilantro, 102
spring 4-day green juice & raw food
    cleanse, 63–90
    day 1, 66–72
    day 2, 73–77
    day 3, 78–83
    day 4, 84–90
    shopping lists, 64, 65
squash
    autumn acorn squash & wheatberry
      salad, 170, 171
    autumn butternut squash with
      spinach, 163
    raw butternut squash soup, 145
stir-fry, Asian, 160, 161
strawberry green juice, 75
summer 4-day green juice & raw food
    cleanse, 91–118
    day 1, 94–99
    day 2, 100–104
    day 3, 105–111
    day 4, 112–118
    shopping lists, 92, 93
summer coleslaw, 104
summer greens smoothie, 30
summer grilled salad, 162
summer quinoa salad, 168, 169
super green juice, 85
super greens & mint salad, 77
sweet collard greens summer salad,
    155
sweet greens juice with ginger, 69
sweet honeydew green juice, 97

sweet nori wraps, 47
Swiss chard
    chard-carrot green juice, 50
    cherry tomato & avocado salad, 99
    nutritional info, 50
    super green juice, 85
    super greens & mint salad, 77
    Swiss chard, 50

tacos, raw guacamole, 135

vanilla-grapefruit green juice, 45
vegan, 5, 11, 23
    vegan Caesar salad, 110, 111

walnut & red cabbage salad, 72
warm spinach & eggs, 165
watercress, 16
    chard-carrot green juice, 50
    cherry tomato and avocado salad,
      99
    honeydew-watercress green juice,
      107
    kiwi green juice, 40
    nutrition info, 46
    simple winter salad, 61
    super greens & mint salad, 77
    watercress arugula salad, 83
    watercress green juice, 46
    winter grapefruit salad, 43
watermelon cucumber salad, 103
winter grapefruit salad, 43
winter green juice, spicy, 52
winter salad, simple, 60, 61
winter sweet potato-asparagus
    casserole, 158, 159
wraps
    almond butter wraps, 42
    collard green wraps, 76
    romaine lettuce wraps, 116, 117
    sweet nori wrap, 47

yellow bell pepper juice, 113
yellow capsicum, 92, 93, 104, 109,
    113, 169

zucchini
    kale-zucchini green juice, 137
    raw zucchini spaghetti, 54
    zucchini-cantaloupe green juice,
      106
    zucchini-pear green juice with
      cilantro, 102